To order additional copies of **We Are the Pathfinders Strong,**
call 1-800-765-6955. For information on other Review and Herald products,
visit us at www.adventistbookcenter.com.

To Tony Hall my friend,
keep trusting !
WO
7/6/00
Toronto, Cnada

WE ARE THE

PATHFINDERS

50

THE FIRST FIFTY YEARS

STRONG

Willie Oliver with Patricia L. Humphrey

REVIEW AND HERALD® PUBLISHING ASSOCIATION
HAGERSTOWN, MD 21740

The author assumes full responsibility for the accuracy of all facts and quotations in this book.

Texts credited to NIV are from the *Holy Bible, New International Version.* Copyright © 1973, 1978, 1984, International Bible Society. Used by permission of Zondervan Bible Publishers.

This book was
Edited by Gerald Wheeler
Designed by Willie S. Duke
Electronic makeup by Shirley M. Bolivar
Cover photography by Joel D. Springer and Steve Rogers
Typeset: 12/14 Bembo

PRINTED IN U.S.A.

04 03 02 01 00   5 4 3 2 1

R&H Cataloging Service
Oliver, Willie
    We are the pathfinders strong, by Willie Oliver with Patricia L. Humphrey.

    1. Pathfinders.   2. Youth—Seventh-day Adventist Church.   I. Humphrey, Patricia L.
II. Title.

                    267.66732

ISBN 0-8280-1498-1

ACKNOWLEDGMENTS

We wish to thank all those who contributed to this book, especially

Daniel L. Davis
Terry Dodge
Mark Ford
Robert Holbrook
Jeannette Johnson
Donald Laing
Norm Middag
Dixie Plata
Elsie Russell
Gerald Wheeler

All these people were also especially helpful in verifying the facts and events presented in this book.

CONTENTS

PREFACE

An old saying states that the youth of today are the church of tomorrow. But not so with the Seventh-day Adventist Church. I'd like to coin a new phrase: The church of yesterday, today, and tomorrow has been, is, and always will be a youthful church. Looking back on our history, even to the very beginnings of the movement, young people have played an important role in the growth and development of our denomination.

Ellen G. White was 17 when she had her first vision. John Loughborough was also 17 when he began to preach the message of Jesus' return. Annie Smith and her brother Uriah were both youth when they joined the Advent movement, and John Andrews at the age of 20 was spreading the message of the Second Coming through the written and spoken word. And the list goes on.

These young people and many others of future generations to whom they would someday pass the torch had (and still have) a vision to share the gospel message with the world. It is a vision that leaves no doubt as to what role the youth of the Adventist Church are to play. Ellen White expressed that vision in these words: "We have an army of youth today who can do much if they are properly directed and encouraged. We want our children to believe the truth. We want them to be blessed of God. We want them to act a part in well-organized plans for helping other youth." And she continued, "With such an army of workers as our youth, rightly trained, might furnish, how soon the message of a crucified, a risen, and soon-coming Saviour might be carried to the whole world!"

She made her statements just before the end of the nineteenth century. Not a single Pathfinder Club existed anywhere. Today, as I look at the vast army of Pathfinders around the world, I wonder if Ellen White could have ever imagined the marvelous way in which her prophetic words would become reality. It is an army of youth filled with a passion for doing, loving, serving, and, most of all, sharing the good news of a Saviour on the verge of His return.

But no army has ever been successful without a staff of well-qualified generals, and this one is no exception. This book honors all the dedicated Pathfinder leaders and pioneers who have unselfishly given their time, talents, and effort without pay—and often without recognition or thanks—to enrich the lives of young people. Why do they do it? Because they, too, have caught the vision so aptly penned in the words of Ellen White. I heartily salute those great men and women of the past, as well as each of you who continue to add to the rich history of Pathfinder ministries today. And may we all give our praise and thanks to the Commander-in-Chief who so nobly leads His army to the finish. It is my hope and prayer that the memories of God's blessings of yesterday will inspire us to even greater heights in Pathfinder ministry tomorrow. Maranatha!

—Willie Oliver
Director of Pathfinder Ministries
North American Division of the
Seventh-day Adventist Church

FOREWORD

It has been 90 years since the establishment of Junior Missionary Volunteer Societies; more than 80 years since the introduction of the Junior Bible Year; more than 75 years since the first summer camps, the introduction of the first Progressive Classes, and the development of the first Vocational Merits; and now it's been 50 years since the Pathfinder Club evolved out of all that and received official recognition by the Seventh-day Adventist Church. In human terms, that's all quite a while ago. During this same time span cars have gone from Model T's to Vipers. Airplanes have evolved from Kitty Hawk to the Concorde. And communication has expanded from telephone to e-mail. The world has seen more and greater changes since World War I than in its entire previous history. Some would claim that we could say it has also been the case since World War II. Yet even World War II now seems to be a terribly long time ago. Most of us alive today were born after "the war," so our memories go back an even shorter time. The novelty of transistor radios, pocket calculators, and 8-track tapes is about as far back as most of us have good, clear recall.

With so many transformations and so much still continually changing, it is easy to completely erase from our minds all that "unnecessary and useless information from the past" and just worry about living in the now. It's all we can do just to keep up with all the novelty and excitement of the moment.

Who cares about all that stuff behind us when even just yesterday is already getting dim? So why print a book about Pathfindering during the past 50 years? Does anybody really care anything about old names and dates—who did what, when, or why?

A famous quote first written by Mrs. Ellen White on December 19, 1892, haunts us with its veracity. She wrote: "As I see what the Lord has wrought, I am filled with astonishment, and with confidence in Christ as leader. We have nothing to fear for the future, except as we shall forget the way the Lord has led us, and His teaching in our past history" (*Life Sketches,* p. 196). Yes, this book is full of names, dates, events, and all other kinds of apparent "trivia" (including a few corrections from past similar materials, thanks to ever-sharpening historical research skills), but through it all, it should help us understand what God has done, how He has led, and then give us confidence in Christ as our personal leader and Master Guide. Enjoy, even reminisce, and give thanks to God.

—*Robert Holbrook*
World Pathfinder Director
of the Seventh-day
Adventist Church

CHAPTER ONE

WE ARE THE PATHFINDERS STRONG!

Discover the Power Camporee

When groups of settlers wanted to move into an uncharted region of the American continent 200 years ago, they hired a guide to take them. Someone who could show them the way through dangerous mountain passes and over raging rivers, and defend them against wild animals. Called Pathfinders, they were the ones out front, ahead of the party, leading the way. And it's no different today.

The Discover the Power Camporee (DTP) was an action event, and it put Pathfinders out in front in a big way. More than a year before the August 10-14, 1999, engagement in Oshkosh, Wisconsin, thousands of Pathfinders from all over the world started getting ready to make the trip. It was the biggest Pathfinder event of the century, and die-hard Pathfinders were determined to be a part of it.

During the six-day event, a group of teenagers and support staff produced a newspaper that chronicled many of the activities that happened there. The following excerpts from that paper represent a cross section of the life and times at the Discover the Power Camporee.

Oshkosh?

The name Oshkosh is well-known by those Pathfinders who once toddled around in the sturdy overalls made there. But when the church announced the location for the 1999 DTP Camporee, most people said, "Where?" Oshkosh may not be a regular crossroads for most people, but it is a long way from being the middle of nowhere.

Oshkosh is the home of the Experimental Aircraft Association, or the EAA. A group of friends who shared the unusual hobby of building airplanes in their garages—homebuilts, they called them—founded the EAA in 1953. Their mission was to make aviation accessible to all who wished to fly. Interest in the EAA soared in 1955 when the founder published an article in *Mechanic's Illustrated* entitled "How to Build an Airplane for Less Than $800, With Engine."

As membership grew, so did the need for more space to hold their events. Their biggest one they called a "fly-in"—an open-air convention where pilots flew their home built planes to a central location where they could show their work, share their problems, and look for solutions. In time, thousands of planes crammed the airfields at the fly-ins until, for safety and convenience, something had to be done. In 1970 the EAA found the ideal setting

A skydiver unfurls the flag of the United States. Photo by Mark Ford.

in the wide open spaces around Oshkosh, Wisconsin. And then things really took off.

Today the EAA has 170,000 members worldwide, and Oshkosh regularly hosts fly-ins attracting more than 12,000 pilots and their planes, and the 800,000 visitors who want to look at them. In 1998 the EAA exhibited 682 home builts, 125 antique planes, 547 warbirds, 38 acrobatic planes, 178 amphibious, float-

A stunt pilot roars low across the EAA airfield in a replica of the famous, and dangerous, GeeBee racer. Photo by Mark Ford.

Ron Whitehead, Camporee director, kept a close eye on operations during the week. Photo by Mark Ford.

of the finest large-scale camping and exhibition facilities in the world. It was the perfect setting for 22,000 Pathfinders to set up temporary housekeeping.[1]

Years of planning and months of hard work made the camporee a reality. It was, for all practical purposes, a city. It had its own radio station, newspaper, post office, police

Pathfinders were treated to an acrobatic demonstration each afternoon. Photo by Mark Ford.

planes and seaplanes, and to top it off, the British Airways' Concorde supersonic airliner. To accommodate them all, the EAA built one

force, hospital, grocery store, and medical clinic. Managing all this was the "mayor," Ron Whitehead from the Center for Youth Evangelism in Berrien Springs, Michigan, and camporee director.

"It's the end of the millenium," he said in one of his many press conferences. "Isn't it appropriate that we are discovering the power of God?"

Debbie Solid, 17, an event staffer from Camp Au Sable in Michigan, is one of many who helped construct the miniature city. "I got lost at least ten times," she said. "But it was an awesome opportunity to witness for God."[2]

Traveling Mercies

From across the continent and around the world, Pathfinders and their clubs came to have fun, meet friends new and old, and in the process tell others about the God they love. Thousands of prayers, asking for travel protection, headed heavenward as Pathfinders traveled to DTP across land and sea. And there were some dramatic answers.

When Pathfinders from the Walla Walla, Washington, Eastgate church left home they had no idea about the miracles and challenges that lay ahead. Just outside of Billings, Montana, their bus broke down. They limped into town only to learn it would cost several thousand dollars to fix it—money they didn't have.

Karen Fishell's 1993 Subaru Loyale was totaled on the way to the camporee. Miraculously, she and her passenger escaped with only minor injuries. Photo courtesy of Karen Fishell.

The local church offered them the use of the school gym for as long as they needed. After talking with their pastor back home, and receiving his support, they decided to somehow continue their trip to DTP.

That Sabbath the Billings church pastor explained the Pathfinders' situation to his congregation. An 84-year-old member felt impressed to help. "I'm getting old and don't need it," he said as he gave them $3,000. It was enough to pay for bus repairs as well as rental cars so they could continue on their way to DTP. "It was a gift from the Lord!" exclaimed the Eastgate leader.

An hour from home, a soft-top carrier containing supplies fell off the top of the van that Grand Junction, Colorado, Pathfinders

Pathfinders of the Many Waters Pathfinder Club from Walla Walla, Washington, arrived safely at Dare to Care, thanks to the generous assistance of a church member in Billings, Montana. Photo by Suzanne Perdew.

were riding in. Staff member Karen Fishell, driving a 1993 Subaru Wagon with her son, Bautch, swerved to miss the carrier. She lost control of the car and skidded into the median where the car rolled over twice. Ambulances took the injured to the hospital, where Bautch received about 12 stitches. Fishell was not seriously injured.

The 17-member group returned to Grand Junction overnight, where church members loaned them a pickup. They arrived in Oshkosh on Tuesday.

"God protected us," says Karen Fishell. "It could have been so much worse. We're very grateful for God's protection. God wanted the kids to come so they could hear all the great stuff and grow in their relationship with God."[3]

In Charlotte, North Carolina, club leader Brian Dudar organized a group of eight Pathfinders and six adults to travel the 1,184 miles to Oshkosh on bicycles. They called their plan "Bike for Life: Teens Against

Tobacco" and turned their trip into a rolling health evangelism program. Dressed in bright orange and black shirts, the teens stressed the message that it's not cool to smoke or use tobacco products to news organizations and church groups along their route.

They left Charlotte on July 18, and pulled into Oshkosh 23 days later amid cheering crowds of well-wishers, local news organizations, and, of course, a Pathfinder color guard. The Northeastern Conference Drum Corps escorted them to their campsite.

"I wanted to be a good witness to other kids that you can keep going," said Josh, one of the youngest bikers whose scraped arms and legs attested to his 14 falls. "I have no regrets

Pathfinders in the "Bike for Life: Teens Against Tobacco" road team pedaled 1,184 miles from Charlotte, North Carolina. Photo by Céleste perrino Walker.

about going on this trip. I would definitely do it again." [4]

Powerful Theme

Among the main attactions for the week were the evening programs held each evening in the main assembly area. As camporee organizers pulled together plans for the evening programs, they wanted a special theme song for the week. After listening to dozens of potential songs prepared by professional recording artists, program coordinator Bernie Anderson decided that the best Pathfinder song could be written only by a Pathfinder.

"DTP was all about empowering kids to go out and do something good for God," he said. "We really felt this was a way to let them share their faith with each other and the world. All they needed was a chance." The church announced a contest for any Pathfinder to submit a theme song that would be sung by 22,000 Pathfinders at the program each evening. The prize was $300.

Valerie Jean Gonzales, 15, and Kristen La Madrid, 14, both from Glendale, California, decided to give it a try. With the encouragement of Valerie's mother, Abigail, who was also the Glendale Filipino Pathfinder leader, they sat at the piano after church one Sabbath and began trying out chords and phrases. They used as their guide the program themes planned for each evening at the camporee. Valerie's uncle, Ruel Banquiero, helped with the recording. With one week to spare before the contest deadline, they mailed their entry. It won.

"Their song really lit up the room the first time we played it," Bernie recalled. "It was unanimous that they had captured the spirit we wanted to share at DTP. It was great."

Valerie and Kristen performed their song, "Discover the Power of the Lord," to an enthusiastic audience on the opening night of the camporee. And people were humming it all week long. It was the kind of song you just couldn't get out of your head.

"The most powerful discovery we can find is the power of the Lord and His love for us," says Valerie. "We wanted the Pathfinders to be able to leave the camporee with a love for Him, something that would never die."[5]

The evening programs were a choreography of light, sound, and . . . electrical cords. Bernie Anderson, backed by a staff of 80 crew members, staged 5 major programs that included music, drama, big-screen video, and live satellite broadcasts, all capped on the final night by a 20-minute fireworks display—firing off more rockets than ever before in the history of Wisconsin.

A crew of 40 people worked two days to build the main stage, the biggest available in the state. Twenty more controlled the stage

Bernie Anderson was the evening program director. Photo by Tompaul Wheeler.

lights and sound, and another 10 helped the actors and performers with makeup and costumes; no small undertaking considering that for the Friday evening performance alone they had 200 props and costumes for actors playing everything from Roman guards to angels. They were picky, too. Sound editors spent 15 hours mixing sound for a two and one-half minute music video.

"We saw it as more of a ministry than a

show," says Bernie. "We carefully planned everything to maximize our technology, and we prayed that the Holy Spirit would move in each night's program. Of course, each program highlighted the Pathfinders' own talents."

The DTP praise team, led by Southern Adventist University chaplain Ken Rogers, started practicing two months before the first program started. "For me, there's nothing more exciting than sharing Jesus through music," says Veruschka Valenzuela, a vocalist from Andrews University. "It's so thrilling to have 20,000 kids join you in singing, 'I believe in God.' We combined a lot of flavors together to make music that everyone could enjoy."

The masters of ceremonies each evening were Tim Nelson and Kevin Bowen. Both 21, they had been friends since fourth grade, "causing shenanigans" they say. But their familiarity paid off.

"We were excited about being there with all those kids," says Tim. "Interacting with them and meeting new people. Praising God with so many people puts us in awe."[6]

Distinctive Settings

Pathfinders set up their tents in an organized chaos all across the 50-acre EAA campground. Club directors and conference leaders went to great effort to make distinctive gateways leading into their respective sites—and some might

think a little competition was in play as well. The colorful and creative decorative constructions ranged from a mock-up of the space shuttle to a scene from the wild wild West.

Del Braman, a retired worker from Atlantic Union College in Lancaster, Massachusetts, made one of the more unusual displays. Building on the theme of Adventist history, Del constructed a model of the meeting house that was home to the first Sabbathkeeping Adventist congregation in the world: the Washington, New Hampshire, Seventh-day Adventist Church, a place where pioneers such

Del Braman from Lancaster, Massachusetts, displays his model of the Washington, New Hampshire, Adventist Church, home of the first Sabbathkeeping Adventist congregation in the world. Photo by Felicia Ford.

as James and Ellen White, John Nevins Andrews, and Uriah Smith all once worshiped.

The five-foot-high model was an exact representation right down to the windowpanes. "It took a month for me to build," Del recalls. "About 140 hours of work by myself. My wife did hold a board or two once in a while," he added, laughing. Del built the church model in his garage at the request of Bill Wood, the youth director for the Atlantic Union. It was constructed in modules that he could disassemble and pack for easy transportation.

"The idea was to touch a new generation of Pathfinders with something of the history of our church," Del explains. "Some of these young people, coming from other parts of the world, are seeing it for the first time. I hope it helps take them back to those early days."[7]

Service

One of the most important goals of the Discover the Power Camporee was to introduce Pathfinders to the many opportunities they have to share the love of God with the world. During the months leading up to the camporee several ministries created custom projects that put the Pathfinders on the cutting edge of service.

Project Air Power

Adventist World Aviation initiated a program for Pathfinders to restore and refurbish a Cessna 182 aircraft now being used in ministry to people living in 50 isolated villages in southern Guyana.

Before the camporee began, Pathfinders from the Morning Star, the Coloma Silver Foxes, and the Niles Four Flags clubs, all from Michigan, put on their oldest clothes, rubber gloves, and protective eye gear to strip paint and clean metal as the first step in a complete overhaul. AWA volunteers removed and repaired the wings, inspected the tail section, re-

The Cessna 182 receives a new engine. Photo by Tompaul Wheeler.

Volunteers working on Project Airpower restored and modified this Cessna 182 for mission service in Guyana. Pathfinders from the Morning Star, Coloma Silver Foxes, and the Niles Four Flags clubs, all from Michigan, assisted in the restoration. Photo by Tompaul Wheeler.

placed control cables, installed new fuel tanks, and made special modifications to the control surfaces that allow the plane to land in small clearings. Other Pathfinders worked to sponsor "shares"—$100 contributions that helped buy the necessary parts and equipment needed to restore the plane.[8]

Project Word

Youth leaders encouraged Pathfinders to collect Bibles from members in their congregations and bring them to Oshkosh. By the end of the week they had delivered more than 150,000 Bibles to the Bible receiving center, four semitrailers side by side that served as the collection depot. But they didn't stay there long. Pathfinders also assisted in packing them for shipment to people who consider a Bible, any Bible, as precious.

"Lots of Bibles sit on shelves not being

used," says Larry Dalson, president of Project Word, who helped coordinate the project. "Many people in developing countries who speak English would love a Bible. We're just shifting the inventory."

Project Word is a nonprofit organization that distributes Bibles and other Adventist literature to developing countries as well as assists in the care of orphans in Haiti.[9]

Larry Dalson, president of Project Word, while constructing the Come Meet the Power superstructure. Photo by Céleste perrino Walker.

ADRA Pack-a-Box

The Adventist Development and Relief Agency (ADRA) set up a packing and shipping center in one of the large hangars at the EAA airfield. As part of ADRA's relief work for the refugees of Kosovo, a Pathfinder could pack a box with school supplies, toiletries, toys, snacks, wash cloths, and pop-up books. ADRA encouraged the Pathfinders to write messages to the Kosovar child who would receive each box. Many clubs made beautiful quilts that they also included, along with clothing collected by Pathfinder clubs prior to the camporee.[10]

Spiritual Celebrities

Pathfinders could meet famous personalities at the Camporee. People like Henry T. Bergh, who helped start some of the first Pathfinder clubs and composed the Pathfinder song; Desmond T. Doss, the Adventist medic who won the Congressional Medal of Honor; and Terry Johnson, the former dyslexic who wound up on the White House Honor Guard. Former world Pathfinder leader Leo Ranzolin as well as current world Pathfinder leader Robert Holbrook participated. World youth leader Baraka G. Muganda and associate youth leader Alfredo Garcia-Marenko also represented the General Conference.

Brandi Chapple was another big hit. As

President Harry Truman presents the Congressional Medal of Honor to Desmond T. Doss on October 12, 1945.

said. "Some people don't see sex as something sacred—they see it as just an act, something to do. I think sex is so precious that no one but the person who is willing to spend the rest of his life with me, can share it with me."

It was a strong message. But Brandi is a strong person, and thinks for herself. "I realized one day that this was really something I wanted for myself. It's so important to live by God's law. People wonder, 'What if God doesn't bless me with the right person?' But if we do things

Brandi Chapple, cohost of BET's *Teen Summit*, tackled tough issues like drugs, family pressures, violence, and fashion.

cohost of *Teen Summit,* a program broadcast worldwide on Black Entertainment Television, or BET, she tackles tough issues such as drugs, family pressures, violence, and fashion. And she has a mission—to help teens make positive choices.

During the camporee her emphasis was on teen sexuality. "Abstinence is the only 100 percent way to avoid pregnancy, sexually transmitted diseases, heartbreak, and more," Brandi

God's way, He'll definitely bless us."[11]

Cheri Peters also knows the value of inner strength. The second child of teenage parents, she endured sexual abuse from infancy on. She first attempted suicide when she was 8 years old by climbing on the roof of her house and jumping off. Homeless at age 12, she became a drug addict in her teens, living off the streets.

At 22 she had had enough, and wanted to die. But as she prepared to attempt suicide again she felt the love of God come over her for the first time. Her transformation began that day. Today, she hosts two television programs and a radio show and helps young people find the love she never felt during her childhood. She lives on a 30-acre ranch in

Krissy Denslow interviews Cheri Peters, host of two popular televison programs and a radio show.

Idaho where troubled teenagers can stay as they overcome their problems.

"The only way to find God is through service," she says. "Any other way is like trying to take swimming lessons through a correspondence course." It was a sentiment right on target at Discover the Power Camporee.[12]

The Sanctuary

When the Israelites back in Bible days went camping, they took their church with them. And something like it was open to all at Oshkosh. The King's Castle exhibit was a reconstruction of what some believe the Tabernacle made by Moses in the wilderness could have looked like. It was an impressive, life-size model complete with Israelite priests, altars, furniture, sheep, and a goat. The structure followed the specifications given in the Bible.

The sanctuary exhibit, built in California by members of the San Diego Clairemont Adventist Church and sponsored by the Omega Broadcasting Corporation, presents a blend of historical fact and theological interpretation. Pastor Ted Tessner, who has spent many years researching the different sanctuary buildings in the Bible, was its director.

"Unless our people understand the sanctuary," he says, "they won't understand the significance of last-day events."

More than 4,000 Pathfinders had the

A full-size replica of the wilderness tabernacle gave Pathfinders an inside look at the foundations of their beliefs. Photo by Suzanne Perdew.

Willie Oliver, NAD Pathfinder director, with three of the baptismal candidates he worked with during the camporee.

The highlight of the week was the baptism service where Pathfinders dedicated their lives to Jesus.

chance to tour the exhibit during the camporee. "I was really impressed with the way they could actually set it up to look like the real thing," said Angela Kast, a member of the White House Patriots from Tennessee. Visitors received response cards at the end of the tour, and more than 100 Pathfinders accepted Christ for the first time after going through the exhibit.

"I got one card that had the greatest quote on it," says Pastor Tessner. "It just said, 'The dude explained it.' I love that."[13]

"Pathfindering doesn't just exist for outdoor skills, or leadership skills," says Ron Whitehead. "Other organizations do that too. Pathfindering exists to point kids to Jesus. We're here to discover the power of Jesus Christ and go to the feet of the true Master Guide."

Candidates in the Discover the Power baptism class show their enthusiasm for Jesus.

[1] Reported by Suzanne Perdew.
[2] Reported by Tompaul Wheeler.
[3] Reported by Tompaul Wheeler and Suzanne Perdew.
[4] Reported by Celeste Perrino Walker.
[5] Reported by Krissy Denslow.
[6] Reported by Tompaul Wheeler.
[7] Reported by Kelli Gauthier and Felicia Ford.
[8] Reported by Suzanne Perdew.
[9] Reported by Celeste Perrino Walker.
[10] Reported by Krissy Denslow.
[11] Reported by Tompaul Wheeler.
[12] Reported by Krissy Denslow.
[13] Reported by Celeste Perrino Walker.

SDA MISSIONARY VOLUNTEERS AROUND THE WORLD

Pathfinders PREPARE

Our Pledge

Loving the Lord Jesus
I promise to take an
active part in the work

CHAPTER TWO

THE SERVANTS OF GOD ARE WE

1950s—and before

July 1950 was a historic moment. Delegates at the General Conference session made the following resolution (see page 30).

"The Junior Missionary Volunteer (JMV) Pathfinder Club is a plan that provides activity and leadership for junior youth the year around. It combines physical recreation with noble ideals. It is the church recognizing the normal hunger of growing youth and supplying a church-centered activity which satisfies this hunger."

And so the Seventh-day Adventist Church officially recognized the Pathfinder organization as a viable entity. But that acceptance did not happen overnight. Nor did the process occur without its challenges and setbacks. To get a full picture of the Pathfinder story we must go back to the very beginning—to Hazelton,

MV PATHFINDER CLUBS:

Recommendations from the Missionary Volunteer Council held in San Francisco were presented, and adopted as follows:

WHEREAS, Many of our larger church community centers are appealing to the Missionary Volunteer Department to provide additional vocational and recreational opportunities in order to profitably employ the energies of hundreds of our boys and girls, in the effort of the church to establish them in the third angel's message; and

WHEREAS, It is highly important that these growing youth engage in church-centered activities which teach the value of character, citizenship and vocational skills,

We recommend, 1. That the Missionary Volunteer organization enter into this expanded activity program under the name of MV Pathfinder clubs.

2. That MV Leaflet 10 be the guide in procedure.

3. That the following points shall characterize the MV Pathfinder Club:

    a. Regular weekly or bimonthly schedule of meetings other than the church school and Sabbath appointments.

    b. Members shall be divided into units with an MV counselor assigned to each unit.

    c. The wearing of the MV uniform shall be encouraged at all appointments.

    d. Hobby classes, recreational events, excursions, camping, and other activities shall be scheduled throughout the year.

    e. Officers of the MV Pathfinder Club shall be elected by the church or churches and shall be designated either as Junior Missionary Volunteer Superintendent or Associate Junior Missionary Volunteer Superintendent.

4. That this MV Pathfinder Club shall in no way supercede any present organization but shall provide additional activity opportunity in those areas where the special need exists.

MV PATHFINDER CLUB—COMMITTEE:

VOTED, That the following be a committee on Pathfinder Club plans, said committee to meet in Denver, Colorado, October 2-5: L. A. Skinner, J. C. Miklos, J. R. Nelson, Henry Bergh, John Hancock, R. A. Nesmith, Lee Carter.

VISITS TO OVERSEAS FIELDS:

VOTED, That we approve of the following visits to overseas fields:

L. K. Dickson, British Union and North Atlantic Division council meetings, September 11-20.

W. P. Bradley, Holland, Scandinavia, and British Union and North Atlantic Division council meetings, August 14-September 30.

E. W. Dunbar, Southern European Division, September 1 to October 15.

E. E. Franklin, Central European Division, publishing institutes, September 15 to October 15.

A. V. Olson and W. E. Phillips, Australasia, November 13 to end of February.

W. E. Nelson and E. E. Cossentine, Inter-American Division for survey of West Indian Training College, August or September.

Figure 1

Cornerstone of Hazelton, Michigan, church.

on that country road they had planted a seed that would some day grow into an awesome army of Seventh-day Adventist Christian youth around the world.

Soon after their little talk with God, the

Warren and Fenner kneeling—beginning of AYS.

Michigan, in the year 1879—when a tiny seed germinated that would one day blossom into a full-fledged organization of young people dedicated to serving Jesus Christ and humanity.

Two boys, 14-year-old Luther Warren and 17-year-old Harry Fenner, felt a burden to reach their unconverted peers. One day as they walked down the road, they talked about Jesus' soon return and wondered what they could do to hasten it. Wanting to do everything they could to help their friends to be ready for the big event, they decided to ask God for direction. "Let's hop over the fence and pray about it," Luther said to Harry. Kneeling under a tree, the two teens prayed for God's wisdom and help in winning their friends to Jesus. Little did those two boys dream that under that tree two boys formed the very first Seventh-day Adventist young people's missionary society. Open only to boys, the group met in Luther's upstairs bedroom for the first few weeks. Right away, they elected a president and a secretary-treasurer, drew up a temperance pledge, and took up an offering to purchase missionary literature. After the first few "band" meetings, as they called them, they invited girls to join.

In 1891 young Meade McGuire, unaware of what had taken place in Hazleton, Michigan, 12 years before, also felt a burden to start a similar organization in Antigo, Wisconsin. "I was but a youth, and had no one to counsel with," he said, "but I felt that something ought to be done to help and inspire the young people. I had never heard of any young people's organization among our people, but acquaintances of mine attended meetings of the local Christian Endeavor Society and the Epworth League. I felt that our own young people needed something of this kind as much as did those of other denominations. I proposed holding a young people's meeting, but my proposal was met with almost universal disapproval. However, the elder, a saintly old man, long since dead, placed his hand on my shoulder and said, 'My boy, you go right ahead. You may have the church for your meeting, and I will stand by you'" (*The MV Story,* pp. 11, 12).

Mead McGuire

It seemed that God's Spirit was beginning to move upon the church to do something for its youth. On December 19, 1892, Ellen White wrote on the subject: "We have an army of youth today who can do much if they are properly directed and encouraged. We want our children to believe the truth. We want them to be blessed of God. We want them to act a part in well-organized plans for helping other youth. Let all be so trained that they may rightly represent the truth, giving the reason of the hope that is within them, and honoring God in any branch of the work where they are qualified to labor" (*General*

Conference Bulletin, Jan. 29, 30, 1893).

Soon afterward several other articles challenged the church and its youth to become more involved in Christian service. Having become acquainted with the Christian Endeavor Society during her stay in Australia, Ellen White was impressed with their activities and enthusiasm for service. Believing that Adventists could benefit from establishing a similar organization, she said, "Let there be a company formed somewhat after the order of the Christian Endeavor Society, and see what can be done by each accountable human agent in watching for and improving opportunities to do work for the Master. He has a vineyard in which everyone can perform good work. Suffering humanity needs help everywhere" (*The MV Story,* p. 15).

Arthur G. Daniels, then president of the Australian Conference and elder of the Adelaide church in Australia, took Mrs. White's counsel to heart and immediately organized a young people's society, the first to be established outside of the United States. The very next year, in 1893, Milton Kern of College View, Nebraska, launched the Young People's Society of Christian Service. And in 1894 Luther Warren organized a Sunshine Band in Alexandria, South Dakota, with the goal "Do something for somebody every day." Its password, "Not I," came from

Galatians 2:20, and their motto was 1 Corinthians 10:31: "Whether therefore ye eat, or drink, or whatsoever ye do, do all to the glory of God."

The idea of little groups caught on, and soon they popped up all over the state. In August 1896 a statewide convention of Sunshine bands convened in Bridgewater, South Dakota, and in 1899 there appeared a small affiliated publication called *Sunshine.*

In April 1899 delegates attending a special conference in Mount Vernon, Ohio, studied Ellen G. White's writings on youth work. Later that year, in August, an organization known as Christian Volunteers formed. The 60 charter members of the organization signed this pledge: "Recognizing the preciousness of God's gift to me, I volunteer for service for Him anywhere in the wide world that His Spirit may lead, and in any form of service that He may direct" (*Missionary Volunteers and Their Work,* p. 15).

Two years later a number of young people's societies organized in Iowa. But it was not until 1901 that the denomination made a concerted effort to establish youth programs on a larger, global scale.

The 1901 General Conference session, held in Battle Creek, Michigan, April 2-23, passed the following recommendation: "We approve the movement to organize Young

People's Societies for more effectual missionary service; and we recommend that a committee of nine or more representative persons be appointed to form a plan of organization and report it to this Conference for consideration" (*ibid.*, p. 17).

Church leadership asked a committee of nine people, including Luther Warren and Flora Plummer, secretary of the General Conference Sabbath School Department, to prepare a plan for the youth program. Their efforts resulted in a proposal that called

➤ for the organization of young people into missionary bands under the leadership of wise adults,

➤ for the *Youth's Instructor* to become the channel of communication for advancing youth activities, and

➤ for the establishment of a committee to "study this work, and push it forward."

Later that year youth activities officially came under the auspices of the Sabbath School Department. By the 1903 General Conference session in Oakland, California, the church could report 186 youth societies with a membership of 3,478 young people (*The MV Story*, p. 26). At the 1905 General Conference session the Sabbath School secretary stated that "since the last General Conference the number of societies has practically doubled, and hundreds of young people who are too far from a society to belong to it or to meet with it, are doing substantial missionary work. At present we have more than 350 well-organized societies, with a membership of fully 5,000. This is the beginning of the 'army of youth who can do much if they are properly directed and encouraged'" (*MVs and Their Work*, p. 21).

When the General Conference Council convened in Gland, Switzerland, in May 1907, the youth program had grown so substantially that the session made the following recommendation:

"Whereas, there are in our ranks many thousands of young people for whom the most earnest and vigorous efforts should be put forth to instruct them fully in the gospel of our Lord, and lead them to give themselves to the work of the third angel's message; and,

"Whereas, the special blessing of God has attended the efforts among our young people put forth under the fostering care of the Sabbath School Department, until it has grown to such an extent that it is difficult for this department to give this work the attention and help which it needs; therefore,

"Resolved, that in order that this work may be properly developed, and thus an army of workers be properly trained for service, a special department, with the necessary officers, be created, the same to be known as the

M. E. Kern

Young People's Department of the General Conference" (*The MV Story,* p. 31).

It marked the official launch of youth ministries in the Seventh-day Adventist Church. Milton E. Kern, a teacher from College View, Nebraska, assumed the chair of the newly formed Seventh-day Adventist Young People's Society of Missionary Volunteers, and Matilda Erickson became department secretary. Kern immediately began to blaze trails in youth programs. Shortly after his appointment, a convention held at Mount Vernon, Ohio, July 10-20, 1907, laid plans for the new organization. Kern summed up the results of

the historical meeting in the following letter, dated July 22, 1959:

"Definite plans were suggested under three categories—Devotional, Education, and Organized Missionary Endeavor. Examples of the Devotional feature were the Bible Year and the Morning Watch. Under Educational we had the Standard of Attainment, which required the passing of examinations in Bible Doctrines and Denominational History, and also selected senior Reading Course books on such subjects as character building, Christian experience, and foreign missions. The Organized Missionary Endeavor included instruction and experience in personal soul winning and other types of missionary work which young people can do" (*ibid.,* p. 39).

The denomination composed membership criteria for the Young People's Society of Seventh-day Adventists and prepared a membership card that included an aim, motto, and pledge for each member to sign.

The guidelines of the society read as follows:

"Object: Association for Bible study and mutual encouragement in every good work.

"Members: Young people who love Jesus and desire to engage in active service in His cause may be members. Membership implies the duty of faithfulness in all that tends to promote the object of the society" (*History of the Seventh-day Adventist Young People's Work,* p. 12).

MEMBERSHIP PLEDGE

L OVING the Lord Jesus, and desiring to cooperate with Him in the closing message of salvation, I promise to take an active part in the work of the Young People's Missionary Volunteer Society, doing what I can to help others and to finish the work of the gospel in all the world.

_____
NAME

_____
ADDRESS

'Enrolled as a member of the

_____Society

_____19____

_____
SECRETARY

Young People's Missionary Volunteer Society

PLAN OF ORGANIZATION

OBJECT.—The object of the Missionary Volunteer Society is association for prayer, Bible study, and missionary work.

MEMBERSHIP.—Those who are members of the Seventh-day Adventist church and are willing to engage in active service for Christ may become members, by vote of the society. Such should sign the membership pledge. Membership implies faithfulness in the meetings and work of the society and in all that tends to promote its object. Members who have not reported missionary work for three months, without some good reason, may be dropped by vote of the executive committee.

OFFICERS AND COMMITTEES.—The officers shall be a leader, assistant leader, and secretary-treasurer. These, with either the church elder, Sabbath-school superintendent, or church librarian, (as the church may choose) shall be an executive committee to plan for the meetings and work of the society. Other officers and committees may be chosen if needed.

ELECTION OF OFFICERS.—The officers shall be elected by the church for a period of six months. The young people should be represented on the church nominating committee.

BANDS.—Societies, especially the larger ones, should be divided into departments, or bands, for different lines of work, such as a Personal Workers' Band, a Christian Help Band, a Correspondence Band, or a Literature Band. Each member should belong to one of these bands. Each member should plan for and do its line of work, and all the members should frequently unite on some one line of work under the leadership of the band representing that work.

MEETINGS.—It is very necessary that the members meet, all together or in groups, to pray and plan for the work. General meetings for all young people and others who desire to attend, will do much to promote the objects of the society. These meetings should usually be held on the Sabbath.

RELATION TO THE CHURCH.—The Missionary Volunteer Society is a department of the church work, and in order that there may be the closest co-operation between this work and the church missionary society, it is recommended that the church appoint a general missionary committee, composed of the church elder, librarian, and Missionary Volunteer leader, to lay general plans for missionary work, the details to be worked out by the respective societies.

REPORTING.—Each member should make a weekly report of work done, and the secretary should report to the Conference Missionary Volunteer Secretary at the close of each quarter.

It is impossible to give a detailed plan of organization which will meet the needs of all churches, because of the different conditions. This general plan should be used with such modifications as are thought necessary to meet local needs.

Membership Card and Plan of Organization

The meeting also established an annual Missionary Volunteer Day and appointed the _Youth's Instructor_ as the official publication. On the first Missionary Volunteer Day, held on March 7, 1908, churches throughout the denomination dedicated their time and attention to the quest of leading young people to their Saviour. An annual offering provided funds to establish Missionary Volunteer libraries in the churches.

Missionary Volunteer Series	Number Fifty-eight

Junior Standard of Attainment Manual

Review and Herald Pub. Assn.
Takoma Park,   Washington, D. C.

Printed in U. S. A.

M. V. LEAFLET 17

The Junior Bible Year

January

1. Gen. 1, 2
2. Gen. 3, 4
3. Gen. 6, 7
4. Gen. 8, 9:1-17
5. Gen. 11:1-9;
   12:1-10
6. Gen. 13
7. Gen. 14
8. Gen. 15
9. Gen. 17:1-5; 18
10. Gen. 19:1-28
11. Gen. 21:1-21;
    22:1-19
12. Gen. 23
13. Gen. 24
14. Gen. 27
15. Gen. 28
16. Gen. 29:1-28;
    31:2, 3, 17, 18
17. Gen. 32
18. Gen. 33
19. Gen. 35:1-20,
    27-29
20. Gen. 37
21. Gen. 39
22. Gen. 40
23. Gen. 41
24. Gen. 42
25. Gen. 43
26. Gen. 44
27. Gen. 45
28. Gen. 46:1-7,
    28-34
29. Gen. 47
30. Gen. 48, 49
31. Gen. 50

February

1. Ex. 1, 2
2. Ex. 3; 4:1-17,
   27-31
3. Ex. 5
4. Ex. 7
5. Ex. 8
6. Ex. 9
7. Ex. 10, 11

February

8. Ex. 12
9. Ex. 13:17-22;
   14
10. Ex. 15
11. Ex. 16
12. Ex. 17
13. Ex. 18
14. Ex. 19
15. Ex. 20
16. Ex. 24
17. Ex. 32
18. Ex. 33
19. Ex. 34:1-14,
    21-35
20. Ex. 35
21. Ex. 40
22. Num. 9:15-23;
    10:29-36
23. Num. 11
24. Num. 12
25. Num. 13
26. Num. 14
27. Num. 16
28. Num. 17

March

1. Num. 20
2. Num. 21
3. Num. 22
4. Num. 23
5. Num. 24
6. Num. 35
7. Deut. 32
8. Deut. 33
9. Deut. 34
10. Joshua 1
11. Joshua 2
12. Joshua 3
13. Joshua 4
14. Joshua 5:10-15;
    6
15. Joshua 7
16. Joshua 8
17. Joshua 24
18. Judges 6
19. Judges 7

In October 1908 the first Junior Reading Course appeared on the scene. It included two books: *Child Life in the Mission Lands* and *Christ Our Saviour*. A pamphlet, "History of the Seventh-day Adventist Young People's Work," written about 1913, stated: "The Reading Course work is a success, and doubtless is destined to become a power for much

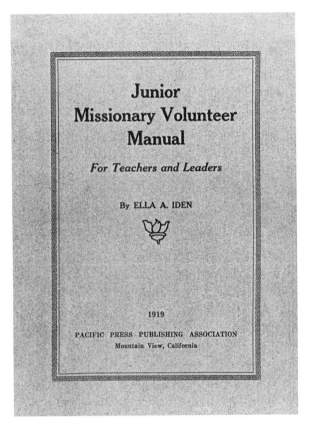

completing the assigned reading in any course and writing the book reviews required, a reading course certificate is granted. During 1912 about 10 times as many reading course certificates were issued as in 1908" (pp. 32, 33).

Rapid growth took place over the next

CONTENTS

good. It is an effort to establish in the lives of our young people the habit of systematic reading of good literature. Thousands of young people and children enroll in the courses, and it is evident that many others read the books without enrolling. The reading circle membership embraces young people in several different countries. . . . To each person

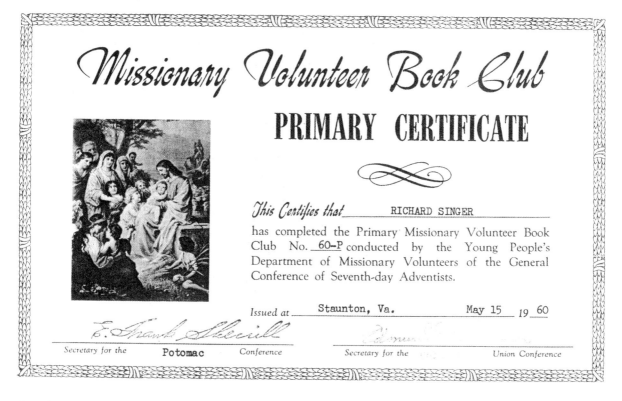

Missionary Volunteer Book Club

PRIMARY CERTIFICATE

This Certifies that RICHARD SINGER

has completed the Primary Missionary Volunteer Book Club No. 60-P conducted by the Young People's Department of Missionary Volunteers of the General Conference of Seventh-day Adventists.

Issued at Staunton, Va. May 15 19 60

E. Frank Sherrill

Secretary for the **Potomac** Conference

Secretary for the Union Conference

decade as several key additions gave impetus and substance to the junior youth program. They included the *Junior Missionary Volunteer Manual,* by Matilda Erickson Andross, in 1913, Junior Society lessons in 1914, Junior Standard of Attainment in 1916, and the Junior Bible year and Primary Reading Course in 1917. By 1919 the denomination had 24,638 members, comprising 1,230 junior and senior societies. Ella Iden-Edwards revised the manual in 1918.

The year 1909, however, was a pivotal one for youth ministries, when the General Conference Session established Junior MV Societies and provided training for Junior MV leaders. From this organization would eventually emerge Pathfindering. Although the denomination would not officially recognize the Pathfinder concept until years later, as early as 1911 the church made sporadic efforts to establish clubs that would meet the unique needs of junior youth. Harold Lewis of Takoma Park, Maryland, initiated one example. Called Pals, it incorporated some of the ideas he had gathered from the Boy Scouts, such as camping and hiking. Two other clubs started in Maryland in those early days. One was known as the Takoma Indians, directed by Charles Boyd. Another was the Woodland Clan. Milton P. Robison formed Boy Pals, a club in Lincoln, Nebraska, whose members engaged in such activities as games, hiking, campfires, and arts and crafts.

The Boy Scouts intrigued Arthur Spalding's two sons, Ronald and Winfred. One Saturday afternoon as the boys and their father passed by a Boy Scout camp, Winfred asked if they could go camping too. Instantly the mental wheels began to turn, and Spalding got the idea to start a club based on similar principles but more in line with Adventist standards. He didn't act on the idea, however, until some time later when he and his sons were doing some gardening. This time Ronald asked if they could go camping. That same evening father and sons made plans for their first outing the following Friday. Several other camping trips followed the first, during which the Mission enjoyed handicrafts, woodcraft, and trailing. In 1919 Spalding started the Mission Scouts for his sons and their Adventist friends.

The foundational principles he incorporated in the JMV pledge and law formed the basis for the pledge and law that Pathfinders still pledge today. The pledge, which encouraged obedience to God and service to humanity, read as follows:

"By the grace of God,
I will be pure, kind, and true;
I will keep the Junior Law;
I will be a servant of God
and a friend to man."

While serving a noble purpose, most of the early clubs involved only boys. The time had not yet come to extend the privileges of club membership to girls. By the 1920s, however, things began to change. In Anaheim, California, John McKim had the opportunity to work with the Boy Scout organization at a very good salary for those days. A Scoutmaster, he was well-equipped for the job. But after prayerful consideration, he realized that any deep involvement with scouting would prevent him from keeping the Sabbath as he should.

Shortly afterward, the Orange County School District offered him a position as janitor, paying a third of what he would have received with the Boy Scouts. He accepted the job, however, knowing that he had made the right decision. In addition to custodial work, his responsibilities at the Lincoln School included taking care of a workroom filled with teacher supplies. He was well-liked, well-organized, and enjoyed his tasks of making the youth and adults around him happy.

The McKims, members of the Anaheim, California, Seventh-day Adventist Church, eventually had a family that included two daughters, Julie and Jean, and a son, Omar.

When Guy Mann became youth director of the Southeastern California Conference in 1927, John shared with Guy his desire to start a program for the youth of the Anaheim church. Together they laid plans for starting a Pathfinder Club that same year.

In recalling the story of the club's beginning, McKim's daughter, Jean Scully, said that she believed the name Pathfinder Club came from an idea her father got at one of the schools. In those days the janitors from each school got together for work bees each summer. The men would go around to each school, sanding down the desks and refinishing them, painting the school, and making necessary repairs. One of the schools in the district, the Fremont school, had been named after the famous explorer and pathfinder, John Fremont. His story impressed McKim, and he told it so often he got the nickname, "Pathfinder." He liked the sound of "Pathfinder" for a club name, as did Guy Mann. So they chose that name for this first conference-sponsored club in southeastern California.

When John McKim and Guy Mann felt the club was ready, they searched for a person to help with the girls in the club. Willa Steen came to mind, as she was quite active in the Sabbath school department at the nearby Fullerton, California, church, where she and her husband, Dr. Claude Steen, attended. So the staff of this first Pathfinder Club consisted of John McKim and Willa Steen and their supportive spouses. They held Friend and Companion classes, did crafts, and organized a youth choir and other activities.

Both the small Fullerton and Anaheim church groups needed more space. So the two groups decided to go together and build one church. In 1929 the club became the Anaheim/Fullerton, California, Pathfinder Club. It met in the public school auditorium where John McKim was custodian and was active from about 1927 to 1935. One of the many projects the group did was community service outreach.

The efforts to establish a more hands-on approach to junior youth work during the decade of the 1920s stemmed from an action by the Fall Council at Indianapolis, Indiana, in 1920 calling for adding "physical and technical training" to the junior youth program. The same council also voted to add a new staff position soon filled by Harriet Holt: junior secretary to the General Conference Missionary

Harriet Holt

Volunteer Department.

A meeting of denominational youth workers in Washington, D.C., the following year passed a resolution calling for "recognizing the active physical nature of the budding youth, their curiosity, their reaching for the ideal, their love of order and ritual, and their easily enlisted sympathies and group cooperation."

The first JMV Progressive Classes formed in 1922 and consisted of four levels of development: Friend, Companion, Comrade, and Master Comrade. At this time JMVs were restructured into a club format that taught students the importance of the JMV law and pledge and encouraged their healthy development on the physical, mental, spiritual, and social levels. At this time the denomination introduced a Comrade Band for teens and leadership development. Both the JMV and Comrade Band organizations had designated uniforms and scarves.

By 1925 a new concept entered the junior youth scene—camping. And it was a good thing. Adventist parents had begun sending their children to non-Adventist camps, but differences regarding such practices as diet and Sabbathkeeping created a conflict for many. The first Adventist camp for youth took place in Australia in 1925, followed a year later by camps for both boys and girls. A camp for boys was held in Town Line Lake, Michigan, under the direction of Grover R. Fattic, youth director for the East Michigan Conference. Harriet Holt conducted a girls' camp in Wisconsin following camp meeting.

The emergence of the junior camp marked the development of an important phase of the JMV program in the lives of the many young people the camps touched. A. W. Spalding defined and noted the significance of the junior camp:

"The Junior Summer Training Camp was, and is, in effect the denomination's camp meeting expressed in terms of junior psychology. Too long the active child and adolescent had been confined to adult forms of religious expression. Now he was given an interpretation of life in active physical recreation and vocational pursuits, mingled and infused with spiritual objectives and exercises. This made the camp thoroughly spiritual in all its activities and service, and joy in religion was keynote. No boy or girl will ever lose the sense of sacredness of the day that began with the Morning Watch on the hilltop and ended at night with the beautiful awe of the campfire, a time of song and storytelling, and the orders of the day, with final prayer" (*The MV Story,* pp. 56, 57).

But as much as the camps turned out to be a blessing, the idea didn't exactly meet with enthusiasm from many church leaders. A *Guide* article that appeared in July 1966 tells the story of the beginning of camping in the Adventist Church:

"The year was 1926. An MV secretary in the East Michigan Conference, Grover Fattic, decided it was time for the Seventh-day Adventist Church to begin a camping program for youth. For churches to sponsor camping was a rather new idea in the United States. Indians and pioneers knew the skills of camping in the outdoors, but organized camping was almost unheard of.

"Elder Fattic had taken a Scout leader's training course and was convinced that camping

had wonderful value for young people. There were many people, however, who were skeptical about such a venture. Why should a church get mixed up in summer camping? What good would that do boys and girls? Sabbath school, church services, and the church school were important, but this idea of 'taking boys and girls out in the woods and turning them loose' was just too much of a departure from anything that had ever been done before."

Fattic wasn't one to give up easily, however. Again and again he asked permission from the East Michigan Conference Committee to sponsor a camp. Finally, the fourth time around, the committee approved his request. But he was on his own as far as funds. If he wanted to engage in such a risky venture, he'd have to find his own resources to finance it. Fortunately, two sympathetic church members donated $100 each for the camp, and with that support, Fattic began his search for a campsite. And in time, the conference did lend their assistance, providing tents for the camp and even supplying the conference truck to transport them. After much preparation, on a beautiful day in June 1926, 18 boys responded to the first line call at Town Line Lake Camp.

"What a time those 18 lads had! They explored the wonders of nature. They hiked, played games, and made interesting crafts to take home to show their parents. Although they didn't know it then, they began a tradition that has been followed in many MV camps ever since—the formation of a 'Polar Bear Club.' When reveille sounded, each camper piled out of bed and ran to the lake for a morning plunge in the cold water. Any boy who was 'chicken' was promptly disciplined by the others. They pulled him out of bed, carried him to the water's edge, and threw him in, pajamas and all! A few times like this and every boy learned he had better not linger after the morning bugle blew!" (*Guide,* July 13, 20, 1966).

The camp was a success despite the fact that a heavy swarm of mosquitos almost stopped it at the beginning. Fattic prayed that if God was pleased with their camp He would drive the pests away. They disappeared for the rest of the week. Then two boys disappeared while playing the game Hide the Flag. Their leader thought disaster had struck, but he found them stuffing themselves in a blueberry patch. The first camp was a success.

The camping idea took off and began to spread. In the West the first junior camp convened in the Southern California Conference at San Gabriel Canyon during the summer of 1928. C. Lester Bond, who became junior secretary of the General Conference MV Department that same year, was an avid promoter of junior camping. During his 18-year tenure as junior secretary, the concept and practice of junior youth camps became well established throughout the denomination. Today, camping remains the cornerstone of the junior youth program.

The first junior camp in Southeastern California Conference also took place in 1928 on a farm at Julian. Boys attended the first week and girls the second. It was only natural for Guy Mann to recruit Willa Steen and John McKim as part of his staff. McKim used his two-week vacation to work at the camps. Other staff members included George Skinner and his son Laurence Skinner.

The General Conference representative at that first camp was A.W. Spalding. A great storyteller, Spalding shared accounts of various men of history, including John Fremont. By then, Guy Mann and John McKim had begun calling their first camp the JMV Pathfinder Camp. The next year, when the denomination purchased its first Adventist youth camp at Idyllwild, California, the name became official when the staff hung up a sign across the entrance that announced: JMV Pathfinder Camp.

Another significant development that took place in 1928 was the introduction of vocational honors to the JMV program. First called vocational merits, then MV honors, and now AY honors, they challenged youth to attain some proficiency in the following areas: automobile repair, bird study, Christian story-telling, colporteuring, cooking, flower study, gardening, health and healing, laundry, art, needlecraft, photography, poultry raising, radio, shoe repair, star study, and tree study. A.W. Spalding and a group of dedicated men and women had written the courses of study at C. Lester Bond's request. Though modified and adapted to fit the changing times, such honors have remained a key feature of the junior youth program through the years. Nineteen new honors joined the list in 1929.

In 1930 the inauguration of the pre-JMV program (now known as Adventurers) gave younger children the opportunity to also join in the fun. It included Busy Bee (first grade), Sunbeam (second grade), Builder (third grade), and Helping Hand (fourth grade).

Also in 1930 a Pathfinder-like activity program began in the Santa Ana, California, home of Dr. Theron and Ethel Johnston, with Lester and Ione Martin assisting them. The group of young people met monthly with McKim's Anaheim Pathfinder club. They also formed the Orange County Choir with Willa Steen as director and Bertha McKim as pianist.

Laurence Skinner, who was assistant youth leader at that time, recalled the events in the establishment of a permanent camp: "In 1930 the Southeastern California Conference purchased a 16-acre parcel of land in Idyllwild, California.

It was a village holiday resort at a 4,500-foot altitude. A large sign was placed at the entrance, announcing, 'JMV Pathfinder Camp.'

"At this time [1932] our Junior Missionary Volunteer Societies functioned with the church schools. A weekly 45-minute period was allotted to the society. The JMV classes—Friend, Companion, and Comrade—were promoted as well as the JMV honors. There were special felt badges given in trees, flowers, birds, insects, cooking, swimming, woodwork, and knot tying. Once or twice a year we would have an investiture service to present the pins and honor badges. I noted that the outdoor requirements in nature and other field events were very difficult. After all, the teachers had to accomplish their work in the classroom. We [felt that we] should have a program apart from the school."

In 1947-1948 in Glendale, California, a youth club organized with Lawrence Paulson as its director. Between the years of 1934 and 1936, Laurence Skinner, who went to Hawaii as island pastor and youth leader, also kept the club idea alive. "While in Hilo, I experimented with an organization of junior youth who met on Sunday and planned hikes and field trips to the volcano area," he wrote. "In 1936 I returned to the mainland as youth leader for Southern California Conference and started a program in Glendale to supplement the church school JMV society. . . . In 1940 I was transferred to Northern California. The enthusiasm for the Pathfinder Club was slowed down by the General Conference youth leadership for fear that the name Pathfinder might cause the MV [Missionary Volunteer] name to fade out.

"I was called [in 1940] to the North Pacific Union as youth leader. In our leadership councils we discussed the possibilities of a Trailblazer Club [a club program that Henry T. Bergh had written and implemented during his tenure in the Pacific Union Conference], but still did not have the General Conference support." In 1946, however, when Laurence A. Skinner moved to Takoma Park, Maryland, to replace C. Lester Bond, the tide began to change. "Eldine W. Dunbar, Theodore E. Lucas, and Laurence A. Skinner, members of the GC Youth Department, authorized the Pacific Union Conference to operate a Pathfinder Club on a trial basis. The North Pacific Union was requested to operate a trial Trailblazers club. The Pacific Union leaders were requested to set the foundation and guidelines for the Pathfinder Club program. The Missionary Volunteer Directors Council members that were involved were John H. Hancock, Southeastern California Conference; Henry T. Bergh, Central California Conference; Clark Smith, Nevada Utah Conference; and Miller Brockett, Southern California Conference, with J. R. Nelson, union youth director. During the meetings the young men broke into small groups to work on various parts of the Pathfinder program. Clark Smith and Henry T. Bergh wrote the first *Pathfinder Drill Manual,* John Hancock and Miller Brockett worked with J. R. Nelson in compiling various 'How to Start a Pathfinder Club' booklets into one."

Henry Bergh tells the history of the Trailblazer club: "About 1943 we sensed a need for a junior youth club in the Portland area, and we organized what we called Trailblazers. We did a lot of the things that Pathfinders do now. . . . We had well over 100 members in it. I was the leader and instrumental in getting that started."

Another key event occurred in 1946 when John Hancock became youth director for the Southeastern California Conference as well as director of the Idyllwild camp. When the camp season was over, a mother came into his office and remarked, "I wish that summer camp could last all year long!" Then the wheels began to turn. Why *can't* summer camp activities and fellowship last all year? Hancock wondered. He tells the story in his own words:

"I was acquainted with [the] Trailblazer Club program—in fact, I had all the organizational plans in my office. I got these out, looked at them, and decided to call Stanley Jefferson, the pastor of the Riverside church, where my wife and I were members. He was a good friend, so I asked, 'Stan, would you be interested in joining me and getting a club going for the boys and girls 10-15 years old in your church?' Stan's response was an enthusiastic *Yes!* You see, his daughter was in that age bracket.

"I consulted with several Master Comrades and others who had helped at Idyllwild, and they offered good counsel and encouraged me to go ahead. So we did. But what would we call such a club? Why, what else in the Southeastern California Conference but a Pathfinder Club? In my ignorance as a new youth director, I didn't know that the General Conference Youth Department did not want the name of JMV to be changed, but I guessed that if [Henry T. Bergh and] Laurence Skinner could have Trailblazers in the North Pacific Union, we certainly could have Pathfinders in our conference, especially since that name was so prominent in youth ministry history" (from *The Pathfinder Story*).

Right away, John Hancock, who had been an art major in college, began designing an emblem for the uniforms that the Pathfinders would wear. Triangular in shape, the three-sided emblem represented three aspects of child development: physical, mental, and spiritual. A shield in the center represented faith in

Jesus, and a sword on top stood for the Word of God. A local embroidery shop made the emblems. Under the direction of Francis Hunt, a college ministerial student, 15 boys and girls, their parents, and other supporting adults led the new Pathfinders in such activities as drills, craft classes, and recreational outings. It was a success from the start. This first-ever conference sponsored group of Pathfinders became a model for an organization of young people that would one day span the globe.

It wasn't long after the establishment of the Riverside club in 1946 that other Pathfinder groups began to mushroom in California. Lawrence Paulson directed one such group based in Glendale, California. Through the years he led 11 different Pathfinder clubs, and, according to John Hancock, was "one of the greatest all-time Pathfinder Club directors in our denomination." Following his death in September 1998, an article in the November issue of the *Pacific Union Recorder* said of Paulson: "Wherever he went Lawrence began a Pathfinder club. He seemed to live, eat, and dream of Pathfindering." In 1947 the Pacific Union Conference officially adopted the Pathfinder Club concept. By the following year Lawrence Paulson's club in Glendale had swelled to 150 members.

The rising popularity of the groups made

such an impact that Skinner, associate youth director of the General Conference at the time, asked the youth department of the Pacific Union to develop the Pathfinder idea as a model for the world church.

During those developmental years several key components of the Pathfinder program emerged. The Central California Conference chose the first area coordinators in 1948. Also in that same year Helen Hobbs sewed the first Pathfinder flag, one based on the design by Henry T. Bergh. And in 1949, at the suggestion of the MV Director's Council, Bergh wrote the "Pathfinder Song."

"I'm no song writer," he responded to the request. "I've never written any songs. I'm not a musician." In a letter written to Michael Stevenson, then World Pathfinder Director in 1984, he said, "I dispatched that idea very quickly. But along in May 1949 I was driving to a Sabbath appointment at Monterey Peninsula from San Jose (70-80 miles away). I was riding along thinking about Pathfinders and about our need for the song and started thinking about a tune. What would be a good tune for a Pathfinder song? Then I thought, *Well, I should write the words.* So I tried to compose a poem. . . . I started thinking of what things I would want to put in the poem for a Pathfinder song. I thought about the MV pledge—'pure and kind and true, with a mes-sage to go the world'—and things started to fall into place. I pulled over to the side of the road, took a piece of paper out of my Bible, and began to write:

"*Well,* I thought, *that's not bad.* . . . I took off again for my Sabbath appointment and got down the road a ways and started to hum a tune. Then I started singing the words with that tune. I have said repeatedly that God gave me the tune, because I am not a musician and I have never written a song before or since. The Lord just gave it to me. I pulled off the side of the road, turned the sheet of paper over, and put down five lines for a staff. I knew enough about music to be able to read it, so I started humming the tune that was going through my mind and putting dots on the staff. . . . That evening when I got home, I asked my wife Miriam to play this thing for me from the dots on the page. We corrected where I had misplaced the dots and got the tune just as it is today. I still wasn't confident that it was good enough for a Pathfinder song, so I sent it to Wayne Hooper, who was a personal friend of ours. I asked Wayne to edit it and to harmonize it. He sent it back and said, 'It's a good song—go ahead and publish it!' So we mimeographed it for use among our Pathfinder Clubs. I think the first time it was really introduced on a conference-wide scale was at the Pathfinder Officer's Convention in

Henry Bergh's original poem for Pathfinder song as written in his Bible.

Ascilimar, California, in January of 1950" (*The Pathfinder Story*, pp. 19, 20).

In 1948 another interesting development took place that would help to shape the direction and purpose of Pathfindering. Several leaders were promoting a merger with scouts. The following excerpt from a letter written by Laurence Skinner affirms God's leading in the movement:

"Representatives of the Boy Scout organization were invited to our office to discuss the proposal that our church authorize the Boy Scouts to operate the program for our junior youth. It was a lively discussion and we assured the Boy Scout officers that we had great re-

spect for their Scout program. [However,] we emphasized the purpose of our church. We believe that Providence has called us to proclaim to the world a Bible message that is not being given by any other church. We believe we have the responsibility to prepare our youth to participate in this proclamation. [We needed to] train the leadership, prepare the books and printed material, develop the uniform with an insignia. The Scout executives agreed that if we could follow this course, they understood our position." We would not be Scouts nor be in competition with them, but would remain separate, friendly organizations, each with our own missions.

Training was also a key development during this period with the emergence of the first Instructors Training Camp in 1949 in the Central California Conference. At the time the General Conference adopted Pathfindering the denomination produced two booklets on the topic. *How to Start a Pathfinder Club* was compiled from booklets written by Henry T. Bergh and Lawrence Paulson, and the *Pathfinder Drill Manual,* by Clark Smith and Henry T. Bergh.

Bergh recounted the story of how the first booklet came about. "Later in the fall I thought we ought to have more material than what I had gotten from Southeastern or Southern conferences. I really don't remember where I wrote and got it, but anyhow we needed more material. So I sat down and wrote 'How to Start a Pathfinder Club.' It survived quite a few printings and revisions through the years, somewhat as I wrote it way back in 1948. With that as my helper I began touring the conference that winter and promoting and organizing Pathfinder Clubs."

Earlier in January the first Pathfinder officers convention met in Ascilimar, California. On September 23, 1951, the very first Pathfinder Fair convened at Dinuba, California. And October 9-11, 1953, the camporee concept began when 55 Pathfinders attended the first-ever Pathfinder camporee sponsored by the Southern New England Conference at Camp Winnekeag in Ashburnham, Massachusetts.

In keeping with the great commission to proclaim the Bible message to friends and neighbors, the first North American Division Youth Congress, held in San Francisco September 3-7, 1947, introduced the slogan "Share Your Faith." Theodore E. Lucas, who coined the slogan, gave simple directions for implementing it: "Begin where you are with what you have." This admonition resulted in the development of a variety of outreach programs for youth, including Operation Fireside, Friendship Teams, Operation Doorbell, Happiness Packages, MV Community Service, and A Treat-Instead-of-a-Trick. The latter program, designed especially for Pathfinders,

had its roots in 1952 in Wisconsin when club members decided to turn Halloween into a witnessing opportunity by giving out pamphlets and collecting canned goods for the needy. The idea spread in popularity, catching the attention of General Conference youth leaders, who endorsed it by providing a special "Halloween and Hope" leaflet for Pathfinders to distribute in their communities.

The leaflet's cover introduced Pathfinders to their neighbors in the following words: "This is the annual visit by the members of the Pathfinder Club of the Seventh-day Adventist Church. We are very much interested in our community, and we decided to celebrate Halloween by bringing *you* a treat. This leaflet tells all about it." Inside, the leaflet offered a biblical explanation of the state of the dead and invited people to enroll in a Bible correspondence course.

As the Pathfinder concept exploded in the church, clubs began to spring up everywhere. It is impossible to trace the movement's growth. In the following pages we will look at some representative examples of how the idea caught on, first in North America and then throughout the world.

Southern New England Conference. Many Pathfinder and youth leaders became involved in these organizations because their own children were participants. The same was true for Pathfinder leader Art Schumaker of South Lancaster, Massachusetts. Art shares some of his earlier memories:

"It was in 1949 and 1950 that Joe Twing was working with Pathfinders and asked if I would join him. One summer, after a few invitations, I finally consented. Pathfinders didn't function as a club during the summer months. But we had a small group of boys who loved to get together for games and swimming, usually at the back side of South Meadow Pond. When we didn't swim, we played games at a tennis court that is now a parking lot.

"I remember Pathfinder leadership training programs held in Bailey Hall on the Southern New England Conference campground. This was to be an outreach program with non-Adventist youth as well as Adventists. Believing this to be a good program and having a son coming of Pathfinder age, I became involved.

"During the 1950s Mrs. Gladys Quitmeyer was elected by the South Lancaster Church to be the Pathfinder director. We organized and had regular staff meetings, which included some of the juniors, to get their ideas on what they would like to do as Pathfinders. Mrs. Quitmeyer is a very talented, capable leader. The name of our club was called 'Nashua,' after the Indian tribe that inhabited this area years

ago. We had our own Nashua club song also, which was composed by one of our staff members. Later we began meeting throughout the summer months for those who cared to come.

"The program was mostly recreational, such as games and corn roasts. We also made occasional trips to Benson's Wild Animal Farm. Once in a while during the school year we would take the group to the Leominster YMCA for swimming lessons—girls one night, boys another.

"Some of the highlights of Pathfindering are Southern New England Conference camporees and Pathfinder fairs. How well do I remember our first camporee one nice cold weekend in October at Camp Winnekeag. We pitched our tents by the lake. Our club used some of the family tents the conference had for camp meeting. I think it was in 1953. The camp had a lot of surplus army sleeping bags. They sure came in handy since it was so cold. We met in the evening at the campfire circle back in the woods. [R. A. Nesmith] was the union youth leader at the time, and in his talk to us he mentioned that he thought it was the first such camporee in the denomination.

"Our second camporee the following year again took place at Camp Winnekeag, and again in the cold fall. We pitched our two-men pup tents by the lake. Due to the cold during this time of year, it was decided that perhaps we should schedule the third camporee for springtime. I believe that one occurred in the month of May.

"Our fairs were held in the gymnasium on the Atlantic Union College campus. Needless to say, our theme was 'Indian Folklore.' Pathfinders acted out some of the skills that the Indians used to do in this area, based on information they gathered from library books. At one of the fairs we started a fire using flint and steel. A couple boys were really good at this. We also had knot tying and first aid.

"Mrs. Quitmeyer served our club well. It was my pleasure to serve as boys' deputy director under her leadership. I was later chosen as the club's director when she resigned.

"My wife and I worked with Pathfinders for many years and thoroughly enjoyed it. It is rewarding to know that many of our juniors of those days are now serving the Lord in many ways. Some are ministers, teachers, doctors, lawyers, nurses, and some are successful business men and women. When I meet them now, they still mention the Pathfinder club. On one occasion, a young man came up to me and said, 'Do you remember me?' I hadn't seen him for years. I said, 'No, I don't.' He said, 'Well, you had me in Pathfinders.' This young man is now a minister in our Southern New England Conference."

Lake Union Conference. Pathfinder history in the Lake Union Conference dates back to the early 1950s. At that time John H. Hancock was youth director of the Lake Union.

The Illinois Conference had clubs at the Danville, Italian Beverly Hills, West Central, North Shore, and Petersburg churches. J. O. Iverson, youth director for the conference, held Pathfinder fairs at Broadview, Illinois, in 1952 and 1953.

Fred Beavon, while pastoring in 1949, started a Pathfinder club in Manistee, Michigan. One of his Pathfinders was a girl named Rose Niesen. As Rose Otis she later became world director of women's ministries at the General Conference and in 1996 the first woman vice president of the North American Division. Elected youth director of the Michigan Conference in 1951, Beavon held an MV Officer's Institute at Emmanuel Missionary College on February 22, 1953, and a Pathfinder fair at Grand Ledge, Michigan on May 17. The first senior camp session at Camp Au Sable took place during 1952. Early clubs included Gobles, Holly, Flint, Kalamazoo, Emmanuel Missionary College, and Manistee. By 1952 the state had 20 clubs, and the number grew to 50 within two years. During the next few years the conference had Pathfinder fairs, camporees, and a Pathfinder congress.

Also in 1953 the Wisconsin Conference had clubs at the Madison, Milwaukee, and

Superior churches. Indiana convened its first Pathfinder Club Institute on February 28 to get a network of clubs started.

Virginia Farnham started the first Pathfinder club of the Lake Region Conference on December 3, 1950, in Midland, Michigan.

African-American Pathfinder Roots. As with all conferences in the North American Division (NAD), Pathfinder ministry in the regional conferences had its beginnings in the Missionary Volunteer (MV) Department and the Progressive Classes. At the time regional conferences formed (1944-1946) the elected MV secretaries such as Monroe Burgess, Addison V. Pinkney, and Jacob Justiss of the original Allegheny Conference, along with Walter Kissack and Leon Davis of Lake Region Conference, Jonathan Roache of Northeastern Conference, Charles Cunningham and Lee Paschal of Southwest Region Conference, Fitzgerald Jenkins of South Atlantic Conference, James Jones of Central States Conference; and Fredrick Slater of South Central Conference all carried the dual responsibilities of educational director and MV secretary.

From very small beginnings the programs, based on progressive class work and with former military servicemen assisting, quickly grew. (At the time of publication the number of African-American Patherfinders totaled more than 16,000, according to James Black,

president of the Black Adventist Youth Director's Association.)

Three African-American clubs organized in the Lake Region Conference area of the union in 1954. They included Shiloh-Chicago, Illinois, under the direction of Earl Calloway; City Temple-Detroit, Michigan, under the direction of Mary Church; and Hyde Park-Hyde Park, Illinois, with A.W. Williams as director.

Leon Davis began the development of the Pathfinder program in the Lake Region Conference through the Missionary Volunteer Department. Pathfinder/youth director Jonathan Roache succeeded him. Other directors made significant contributions to the Pathfinder program in the conference. At the time of publication Pathfinder coordinator Robert E. Johnson, a Master Guide and Pathfinder leader for 24 years, continues in the Lake Region Conference. He is recognized throughout the conference for creating and implementing Lake Region's Pathfinder patch. Johnson also developed the "Francis Clipper" newsletter and the cartoon character "Willy the Worm." Assisted by a number of leaders and Pathfinder workers, he and his team are working hard to train new Pathfinder leaders to carry the conference into the twenty-first century.

In the overall development of African-

American Pathfinders, though, two individuals especially stand out: Eva Gibbs Strothers and Daniel L. Davis.

Eva Gibbs Strother (1906-1992). Mrs. Eva Gibbs Strother was a youth and Pathfinder leader for more than 57 years. In 1933 she became the Junior MV Society leader for the Ephesus church in Harlem, New York. She led the first group of Black Adventist youth to be invested as Junior Missionary Volunteers in 1935 when she was invested as a Master Comrade by John Hancock.

Eva also directed the first Black junior camp at Verplank, New York, in 1936. Later she bought this campground with her own money, and it remained the Pathfinder campground for many years. In 1936 Eva married Jake Strother, who helped her with Pathfinder activities until he died in 1979.

She worked as a Pathfinder leader alongside Jonathan Roache, and later Leon Davis, both youth leaders in the Northeastern Conference, until 1968 when the Strothers moved to Sacramento, California. Then in 1972 Eva moved to Huntsville, Alabama, where she helped with the Pathfinders of the Oakwood College church until 1985, at which time she became the Pathfinder leader of the Mount Calvary church.

During her ministry, Eva Strother earned two sashes of honor patches. She spent much of her own money for uniforms, trips, and whatever else she felt her Pathfinders needed and deserved. Needless to say, Eva had countless Pathfinder members who went on to greatness during her 59 years of service. Among them were Charles E. Bradford, Benjamin Reaves, and Calvin B. Rock. Eva always looked forward to attending the Northeastern camp meetings each year where she would meet her former Pathfinders and their children and grandchildren.

Daniel L. Davis. Former MV-AY-Pathfinder director of the original Allegheny Conference and then of Allegheny East Conference, Columbia Union Conference, and the Africa-Indian Ocean Division, Daniel Davis was a strong contributor to the African-American Pathfinder movement as well as Pathfinders in general.

During the fall of 1963 church administration asked him to leave the pastoral/evangelistic ministry to become a youth specialist. His new role encompassed Missionary Volunteer services, temperance activities, and the National Service Organization.

In 1963 Davis found only three or four fledgling clubs in all of the Allegheny Conference. They had been organized and chartered by A. V. Pickney and Jacob Justiss, former youth directors in the early 1950s. The clubs included a Washington, D.C., area combined club sponsored by the Alexandria SDA Church, and the Ephesus church (now known as the Dupont Park SDA Church). Laertes Gillis, who was recently out of the Army and Civil Air Patrol, served as leader. The Ebenezer church of Philadelphia, Pennsylvania, had a club led by Ervin T. Glenn, another returned soldier. The other two clubs were from the Glenville (Cleveland, Ohio) and the Newark-Montclair, New Jersey, churches.

Danny Davis (as he is fondly called) recalls some of the events that put African-American Pathfinders on the map. "Upon learning of the Columbia Union-wide camporee that was being planned for 1965 at Swallow Falls, Maryland, we visited and encouraged churches to become involved in Path-finding. The existing clubs grew in membership, new clubs formed, and we finally had representation at this major event. I had appointed Laertes Gillis as the first conference-wide Pathfinder coordinator. Leon Trusty, who succeeded him as director of the First SDA Church Pathfinders, brought our largest group. John Hall, of Pittsburgh, Pennsylvania's Ethan Temple, had a unit of seven boys. Glenville-Cleveland's girls drill team gave a very impressive performance. The Pine Forge Bulldogs, an all-boys unit, were sharp and did extremely well. Northern New Jersey sent a club from Montclair-Newark. A small group came from Philadelphia-Ebenezer. There was no overt competition as we have now, but I believe that these four Allegheny clubs were as good as any registered there.

"Shortly after returning from the camporee at Swallow Falls, Maryland, God gave us the idea that camp meeting would be an ideal time to showcase Pathfinders. Our conference officers, W. L. Cheatham and W. A. Thompson, gave us the green light, and now members of churches who had never thought of Pathfinders before, now marvel at the skills attained and the character traits displayed by these trained young people, and asked for us to form clubs for their children in their own churches.

"Taking an organizational page from our thriving Senior MV Federation program, we

Regional conferences were active in can collecting.

elected Pathfinder coordinators from each area and specialists for various categories. Incidently, the recently-elected mayor of Philadelphia, Pennsylvania, John Street, was president of the Senior MV Federation program as well as a Master Guide and Pathfinder counselor. All these leaders cooperated with the conference Pathfinder coordinators and myself, the conference youth director.

"Shortly after Allegheny Conference divided into Allegheny East Conference and Allegheny West Conference, this staff became a teaching team who, over the years, have traveled to at least five different unions in North America to help train hundreds of Patherfinder staff members in at least 12 conferences. Some team members, such as Ervin T. Glenn, Merwyn Arms, Charles Cason, Euliss Bailey, and James Street have served on union and General Conference Pathfinder advisory committees, and have made significant contributions to the Pathfinder program.

"While I was with Allegheny East," Davis remembers, "we initiated the first international overseas camporees: Bermuda at Ferry Reach, and then in cooperation with Northeastern's Pathfinder director, George Timpson, one in Trinidad-Tobago. Also during this period Allegheny East Pathfinders became well-known for a number of innovative activities, such as subway-stop witnessing, street witnessing, park rallies, Better Living and Temperance parades in the downtown areas of major cities, and drum corps in most of the major clubs. Phazz 1 was an outstanding drill and performance organization of teen Pathfinders.

"The 100-member drum corps, composed of some of the best drummers from all over the conference, played a significant role in publicizing our church as it represented Adventists in many major or even national events.

"They included: the official opening ceremonies of the North American Olympic gymnastic trials in Michigan; the official opening ceremonies of the new General Conference headquarters building in Silver Spring, Maryland; and serving as the official representatives of Maryland's governor in a nationally televised Fourth of July parade in Washington, D. C.

"One little-known historical fact of the late 1960s is that Pathfinder leadership saved Takoma Park and the General Conference from possible destruction during the riots that erupted after the assassination of Martin Luther King, Jr. One evening during the riots a group of us were standing on the sidewalk in front of First church. We included: C. C. Weis, then Columbia Union lay activities director; E. E. Cleveland, associate director of the General Conference Ministerial Association; Laertes Gillis, Pathfinder coordinator of the Allegheny

East Conference; Charles Cason; Leon Trusty, Pathfinder director of First church; my wife, Elizabeth; and me. As we stood there, four men approached us. Immediately we knew that they were community activists and leaders.

"'You people are doing a good job,' they told us pointedly. 'You have made us change our minds. We were ready to burn down Takoma Park next! But because of what you're doing in the community, we won't. Keep it up.'

"My wife and I had been on the way to an MV Council when we heard over the car radio about the start of the riots. I immediately called the Allegheny East and Columbia Union Conference offices, but could not get through. Finally I reached E. E. Cleveland, who had just reached Washington. 'Danny, Washington is burning!' he told me. 'Man, get back here!'

"Because I held both the offices of Lay Activity (now Community Services director) and Youth (MV) director, and knowing the leadership style of our First church Pathfinder leader, Leon Trusty, I immediately telephoned him to get things organized. 'Chief, we are already rolling,' he told me. Then I started on my way back to D.C.

"Luckily, I had both my uniforms with me, because when I reached Washington, I discovered that no one could enter the city without official clearance. Military police and Washington, D.C., officers were everywhere. They searched every car for bombs or weapons. It seemed that the only vehicles moving around the city were Army, District of Columbia. police, emergency services, or private ones labeled as Seventh-day Adventist. When we drove into the fire-ravaged area of northwest Washington, we found that First church, located in the devastated area, had been designated an official headquarters and an emergency supplies distribution center.

"Since it was not safe in the neighborhood for non-African-Americans, the churches of the Potomac and Chesapeake conferences worked through our local churches. The Red Cross, Salvation Army, governmental agencies, and other organizations funneled supplies to First church for us to distribute. Our Pathfinders, Dorcas women, and Adventist Men personnel handled blankets, food, clothing, and other items. We utilized even younger Pathfinders of all three area conferences to sort clothes, fold blankets, pack food boxes, and load Seventh-day Adventist vehicles to send to First church, which had been designated as a distribution center and was a beehive of activity. Carl C. Weis, lay activities and welfare director of the Columbia Union Conference, worked with R. H. Broderson, lay activities director of the Potomac Conference, to borrow an 18-wheel tractor-trailer rig from the New Jersey Conference.

"Staffed by older Allegheny East Pathfinders as well as Pathfinder leaders and Adventist men from the First and Dupont Park churches, trucks, vans, and cars prominently identified as either belonging to a Seventh-day Adventist institution or marked as 'SDA Health and Welfare' went up and down the streets distributing needed supplies. First church registered and assisted more than 11,000 people. The four men who later met us in front of First church knew what we were doing, and expressed their appreciation for it. Pathfinders had been a prominent part of the project.

"We know of none of our people who were hurt or harmed. Once E. E. Cleveland was almost in the line of fire of a sniper's bullet. He had been talking to a non-African-American taxi driver when the military police chased them away from the area. Another time my wife and I drove Carl C. Weis back to the union office in Takoma Park. We made him lie down on the back seat of our car to get him safely through the riot-torn area.

"So we can see that Pathfinder organization, training, and leadership, has made a big difference, and played a major role in the Columbia Union. From the relatively few Pathfinders in Allegheny when I began my ministry, they grew to 3,300 when I went to the Columbia Union. Allegheny West had almost 1,000 at that time."

Spanish-speaking Club. The first Spanish-speaking club began in 1955 with Sally Torres and Connie Perez in the Santa Ana, California, Spanish Church. Connie recounts some of the club's history and memorable experiences:

"The month before we started, Sally broke her leg and was unable to continue directing the club. We had just purchased a church on Third and Shelton streets, close to the center of town. Pastor Eliezer Benavides was our pastor. We have never been without a club since our first Tuesday meeting in September of 1955.

"In November 1958 we participated in the Santa Ana Victoria parade. We also marched in the annual Christmas parades until they started having them on Saturdays in 1967. Our club received several trophies.

"Lawrence Paulson went with us on our first camping trip to Forest Falls in the San Bernardino Mountains, where we went on a night hike up the waterfalls using flashlights. We had no equipment for this trip, so Lawrence went with me to an army surplus store where he helped me obtain tents and other things. Twenty-four Pathfinders were in our group, and they have never forgotten that night. The children and grandchildren of these Pathfinders are a part of the club today.

"Bill Dopp, Southeastern California Conference youth director, enabled us to start a drum and bugle corps by helping us find the instruments. We again participated in parades at San Diego Academy, Lynwood Academy, and many other places. Magadalena Bush and Pastor Robert Taylor from the Good Samaritan church joined us in the project. We practiced every Sunday with between 50 and 60 Pathfinders. Also we had a group of girls who did flag twirling.

"In 1975 I was chosen to be the first female area coordinator, so some of the former Pathfinders took over the leadership of the Santa Ana Spanish Club. The Garden Grove Spanish Pathfinder Club, led by Roger Perez and Tom Sanchez (former Pathfinder members of the Santa Ana Spanish Club) were so excited about Camp Hale that they put their groups to work in every way they could think of to earn money to attend the camp. They had no place to meet, so they made a meeting place in one of the rooms of the DBS Wood Products warehouse. They used this warehouse for nearly three years, taking full advantage of the large amount of space to play basketball, skate, and drill without having to worry about the rain.

"Through the years the Spanish churches in the Southeastern California Conference were quite interested in getting clubs started. As our churches grew, other congregations started in Anaheim, La Habra, Costa Mesa, Garden Grove, and Santa Ana Bilingual.

Pathfinders who became members of these churches started clubs there. Lawrence Paulson and Rose Martinez organized the Redlands Spanish Church's Pathfinder Club. Several churches asked me to help them start a club because I was bilingual. Calexico, San Bernardino, Vista, San Diego, and Tijuana, Mexico, are some of the clubs I assisted. Ninety-eight percent of our Spanish churches have Pathfinder clubs in the Southeastern California Conference."

Hawaiian Islands. Rumors of an organization called Pathfinders traveled to the Hawaiian Islands and in May 1950, dedicated laymen, with the help of General Conference representative John F. Knipschild, laid the foundation for this new organization. Rita K. Martin coordinated Hawaii's Pathfinders for 28 years until 1995. Other individuals who contributed to Hawaii's Pathfinder beginnings were Joyce Villegas, Jimmy Chong, Helen Aladen, Rasalind K. Chang, Irene Kobashigawa, Bill Villegas, Alfred Dhow, and Kenneth Fujimolo.

Among Hawaii's first organized clubs were the Aica, Honolulu Central, Kaiba, and Diamond Head groups. Forty-five years later the list grew to include Filipino Affiliate, Manoa Japanese, Samoa Tokekan, Hilo, Kona, Molokai, Kaneobe, Wahiawa, Waianae, and Waipabu. Initially, the clubs "offered the Missionary Volunteer program to learn how to serve others and to strengthen their own dependence on a loving Saviour," Martin recalled.

By the end of their first year, they had a jamboree at the McKinley High School, across the street from the old conference office building in Honolulu. International flags decorated the auditorium and club booths. Harry Garlick, a Pacific Union youth leader, filmed the marching drill which had military officers judging the participants. The Aica Club won the first place trophy.

On August 19 and 20, 1995, Pathfinders from throughout Hawaii gathered in Honolulu to celebrate 45 years of Pathfindering in the island state. Today, club objectives have not changed. "Our children are our greatest treasures," Martin stresses.

When in 1950 the General Conference officially authorized JMV Pathfinder clubs, the news spread rapidly. The Pathfinder Club concept of involving young people in all sorts of special activities attracted interest in many parts of the world. Here is a glimpse of events and facts that have helped to shape Pathfinders' worldwide existence.

South America

When the exciting news reached the Miraflores Adventist Church near Lima, Peru, South America, several youth leaders decided that it was time for their youth to join the realm of Pathfindering. Under the encouragement and leadership of J. Von Pohle, who was at that time youth director of the Inca Union, the Miraflores congregation formed the first Pathfinder club in Peru. Mrs. Nercida de Ruiz assumed the role of club director along with her husband Armando and several other youth leaders: Mrs. Phil, Segundo Guerra, Moises Rojas, Leonardo Pinedo, and Mrs. Ruf.

History was in the making. Nercida was not only the club's first director, but also the first Pathfinder club director in South America. The club named itself Conquistadores (Conquerors) in recognition of the youths' plan to "conquer" the world for Christ, "conquer" new friends, and "conquer" the kingdom of heaven. Some discrepancy exists as to exactly what year the club actually began. Some say it started in 1955, others 1956.

In 1957 Pastor Jairo Araújo, South American Division youth secretary, prepared a handbook to teach how to start a Pathfinder Club. South America conducted its first investiture in 1958. One year later Pastor Wilson Sarli established the first official club in Riberão Preto, of which Edgar Turcilio became the director, then later Luis Robert Freitas.

South Pacific

A. G. Daniells developed youth clubs in

Australia as early as 1892. In 1953 Kevin Silva, inspired by what he had read about the American Pathfinder program, trained a group of youth at the Preston church in Melbourne and founded South Pacific Division's first Pathfinder Club. The Preston Club exhibited a hobby display and staged a Pathfinder parade at the Victorian Camp session in February 1954—the first such parade in Australia.

Pastor L. Hay conducted a Pathfinder counselor's camp at Eagle Hawk Neck, Tasmania, June 11-14, 1954. Fifteen counselors and leaders came together to study the impact Pathfindering might have on local churches. By October 28 that same year Australian young people had their first Pathfinder Fair at Adelaide's Centennial Hall under the direction of Pastor W. Rudge.

In 1959 the Victoria Conference boasted 18 clubs, 150 directors, and nearly 600 Pathfinders. Nineteen years later Victoria had 24 active clubs.

Several clubs branched off from the Preston Club. One of them, Greensborough, had only six members when it began. Because Greenborough did not have a church building at that time, the club met in the homes of the Ellis, Haysoms, and Wilson families. By 1962 the congregation had built a church.

Years later, in 1975, the youth in the Yarramundi and Greensborough clubs re-ceived merit awards, many on advanced levels. They also received six Silver awards and every member, including Master Guides, were invested.

The Pitcairn Island Pathfinder Club began October 12, 1964. The club recessed for a while and later revived in 1972, when the 18-member club had its first campout.

CHAPTER THREE

FAITHFUL AS WE MARCH ALONG

1960s

April 11-14, 1960, the Pacific Union Conference held the first-ever union camporee in Lone Pine, California. Two years later, the first *MV Pathfinder Field Guide* came off the press. The guide, the product of numerous committees and individuals and edited by Lawrence Maxwell, provided an instruction manual for nature and outdoor activities.

Pastor Joel Sarli, education and youth director of the Paulista Conference, met John B. Youngberg during a 1961 youth congress in Cordoba, Argentina. Youngberg, until recently professor of religious education in the school of education at Andrews University, was responsible for developing Chile's Pathfinder club and first training camp. Inspired by the encounter, Sarli started the Capão Redondo Club in São Paulo.

MV Pathfinder Field Guide

teach various honors and conduct classes as well as serve as unit counselors. It strengthened the Pathfinder Club while giving youth a chance both to lead juniors and to stay involved in the Pathfinder Club past eighth grade.

The Teen Pathfinder program really took off in the Southeastern California Conference where teens literally ran some clubs. One such club in Loma Linda, California, had, at one time, more than 45 teens working with more than 150 Pathfinders. The teens planned such activities as campouts and Sabbath and mission activities. Many conferences across the North American Division had yearly training sessions for their teens. They also offered annual award trips, such as Southeastern California's trip on the Colorado River, and Columbia Union's award canoe trip to the Algonquin Provincial Park in Canada.

Pathfinders participated in a youth congress at the Long Beach, California, Sports Arena, April 11-13, 1963. More than 10,000 young people attended the event. Pathfinders displayed floats in the Friday afternoon Youth on Parade. Speakers included Olympic champion Rafer Johnson, H.M.S. Richards, and radio newscaster Paul Harvey. The Youth Congress also conducted an Investiture for more than 1,200 Master Guides.

In 1962 Norm Middag, while working in the Northern California Conference under the direction of youth director Jim Harris, wrote the first teen program for older Pathfinder youth. Called Teen Counselors, it was a hands-on training approach that prepared teens to

In 1964 Merrill Fleming began a 26-year tenure as Pathfinder director of the Michigan

As an incentive, teen counselors went on special award trips such as this one.

Conference. Graduating from Emmanuel Missionary College in 1952, he began his career as a teacher. While teaching grades 5-8 at the Gobles, Michigan, church, he was active in the local Pathfinder Club. Next entering the pastorate, he continued to be involved in Pathfindering. After pastoring the Niles, Michigan, church and helping lead the Niles Four Flags Club, he went to the Michigan Conference office where he set a record as the longest serving Pathfinder director. During his years as director he built the nature center at

Camp Au Sable in Grayling, Michigan. Fleming would retire in 1990.

Austrian Union of Churches. After World War II many in Europe strongly opposed everything that even resembled a uniform. In the early 1960s, despite these rejections, the Austria Union's former youth director Josef Stoeger made some initiatives toward establishing new Pathfinder clubs. It took several years for the idea to take hold, and in 1967 Walter Schultschik, youth director at that time, officially established the Pathfinder idea—complete with uniforms—and started the Austrian Union's first training seminars for Pathfinder leaders.

From its small beginnings the Pathfinder organization quickly grew into one of the most active and effective programs for youth in the Seventh-day Adventist Church. Its goals remain much the same today: to lead young people into a meaningful relationship with their Saviour, to involve them in service for others, and to challenge them to become responsible, mature individuals who make decisions on the basis of Bible principles.

As Norm Middag, former director of NAD Pathfinder ministries, so aptly puts it, the purpose of Pathfindering is "to improve the lifestyle of the Pathfinder-age young person and to place him or her in the mainstream of the church. We want to help the Pathfinder gain a sense of belonging in the church by taking an active role in fellowship, worship, outreach, and service; to involve the Pathfinder as a full member of the church, carrying significant responsibilities; and to challenge the Pathfinder in the mission and ministry of Christ, so that life becomes meaningful and fruitful for Christ. This is the purpose of the Pathfinder organization."

The Pathfinder Club

The Pathfinder Club includes three phases of ministry: junior, teen, and leadership training. Pathfinder Club members consist of young people in grades 5-10 who meet for regular club activities, such as progressive class work; honors; camping, nature, and recreational activities; marching and drilling; field trips; fund-raising projects; community service; and evangelistic outreach. Each meeting begins with a short ceremony in which youth sing the Pathfinder song and recite the Pathfinder pledge and law.

The club staff includes a director who, often as a Master Guide, supervises the club activities and is assisted by a deputy director and Pathfinder counselors, some of whom are older youth. The staff must attend a basic training seminar on Pathfinder ministry. To become a Master Guide one must be at least 16 years old and a baptized member of the Seventh-day Adventist Church. In addition, Master Guides must participate in in-service training, gain experience in leading a variety of youth activities, have a knowledge and understanding of child development, and develop skills in the areas of leadership, communication, camping, resource development, and child and youth evangelism. They must also engage in personal and spiritual development and study Scripture, the writings of Ellen G. White, denominational history, and church doctrine. Also, they need to acquire personal skills and understand child and leadership development.

Pathfinder Law

Keep the Morning Watch.
Do my honest part.
Care for my body.
Keep a level eye.
Be courteous and obedient.
Walk softly in the sanctuary.
Keep a song in my heart.
Go on God's errands.

The Pathfinder uniform may differ in color and appearance from country to country, but regardless of where they live, or the style of uniform they proudly don, Pathfinders everywhere are united by a common aim. Every aspect of the Pathfinder emblem has a symbolic meaning, representing the Christian values that Pathfindering seeks to instill in young people.

The Pathfinder Emblem

The red of the Pathfinder emblem points to the sacrifice Jesus made for our salvation. The white stands for purity and the righteousness of Christ that we desire to have in our lives. Blue stands for loyalty. Pathfinders strive to be loyal to God, their parents, and the church. Gold symbolizes excellence as Pathfinders aim to reach high standards of character. The three sides depict completeness, as represented in the Godhead. All Pathfinder activities develop the mental, the physical, and the spiritual sides of the person. The shield reminds us of the protection of God's Word, while the sword represents God's Word as we battle against the enemy.

Pathfinder Flag

The Pathfinder flag designed by Henry T. Bergh in 1948 is still in use today. The flag's colors are also symbolic: blue for courage and loyalty and white for purity.

Pathfinder Activities

Bible Bowls. Pathfinder Bible bowls are annual events in North America to increase the young people's Bible knowledge and to gain a closer relationship with Jesus. Both Trevor Baker of the Northeastern Conference and Terry Dodge have spearheaded the concept. Each year Pathfinder leadership chooses a specific portion of the Bible (usually a book of the Bible) from which to select Bible bowl questions. A Bible bowl has no losers. Each participant receives a prize according to his or her knowledge.

Evangelism and Witnessing. A major component of Pathfindering is witnessing and

evangelistic activities. We can trace many baptisms directly to the efforts of Pathfinders who seek through a variety of creative activities to share their faith and reach friends and neighbors with the gospel. These include, to name a few, participation in Revelation seminars, children's evangelistic meetings, clown and puppet ministries, short-term mission trips, youth rallies, anti-drug marches, musical programs, door-to-door visitation, literature distribution, and involving non–Adventist youth in club activities. Many conduct Voice of Youth junior evangelistic meetings and take part in the Pathfinder Evangelism Award program. Youth who participate for a certain number of nights during evangelistic meetings receive a special patch.

Service/Outreach Activities. Hand-in-hand with evangelism go such service activities as food collection and distribution, homeless ministries, soup kitchens, yard work for the elderly, adopt-a-grandparent programs, roadside and park cleanup, assisting local community service organizations, serving as church deacons/deaconesses on Sabbath, and organizing Sunshine bands to minister to residents of local nursing homes.

Pinewood Derbies. One of the most popular club activities has been the Pinewood Derby. Pathfinders carve little wooden racing cars from a small block of wood or special kits. Then clubs gather at least once a year to race them down a special ramp. Many clubs will have a pre-racing event to prepare for the derby itself. The derby will be either at a Pathfinder Fair or a special Pinewood Derby

Clubs enjoyed having their picture taken with the food cans they collected for needy families.

day. The little cars roll down the ramp, propelled only by gravity. Pathfinders often like to decorate the vehicles. Making the cars challenges creativity as well as skill. The derbies will give awards both for the fastest cars and the most imaginative.

Bikeathons. In these conference-sponsored events, Pathfinders spend a day of challenge and adventure in riding their bikes for fundraising and fellowship. Sponsors donate funds to riders based on the number of miles they ride, and the money they earn helps to finance local club activities.

Other examples of fundraising activities

Drill team

Knot-tying was a popular activity at Pathfinder fairs.

Pathfinders engage in include hosting garage sales, talent shows, dinners, car washes, fruit sales, harvest festivals, and producing and selling cookbooks.

Pathfinder Fairs. These are annual events in which clubs from all around the local conference get together for craft and nature activity exhibits, parades, and demonstrations. Many clubs sell food as a fund-raising project. Such events have good attendance by church and community members alike, and provide an opportunity for Pathfinders to display their knowledge and skill. A number of conferences have the first Sunday of camp meeting as Pathfinder Day or Pathfinder Fair Day.

Drill Teams and Drum Corps. One of Path-

Drum corps

findering's most spectacular activities is the drill team. The teams perform publicly and demonstrate their precision skills in marching and drilling. Drum corps often accompany the Pathfinder drill teams.

Camporees. These conference-, union-, or division-sponsored events enable clubs to spend a weekend together outdoors. Club members sleep in tents, prepare their own meals, develop outdoor survival skills, and engage in a variety of nature and recreational activities. The highlight of the camping experience is the evening campfire program

designed to lead youth into a love relationship with Jesus. Individual clubs also sponsor periodic camping trips during which Pathfinders engage in similar activities on a smaller scale.

Pathfinder Day joined the church calendar in 1957, and churches usually observe it the second Sabbath of November. It gives the Pathfinder Club recognition, informs the church of its objectives and accomplishments, recruits adult members of the church as counselors, and encourages all boys and girls who are not yet members to join. The Pathfinders attend church in uniform. They sit together as a group, display the flag and guidons, and participate in the special worship service with their directors and counselors.

AY Honors. The Honors program, which made its first appearance in 1928 for the MV and JMV programs, today remains a cornerstone of Pathfindering. Known as MV Honors up to 1979, it is a hands-on activity designed to help youth develop skill and proficiency in several categories, including arts and crafts, health and science, household arts, mechanics, missionary endeavor, nature study, outdoor industries, and recreational pursuits. The skills learned in the honors program not only help to channel the creative energies of young people, but are a key component for the development of Christian character. When a Pathfinder meets the requirements for an AY Honor, he or she receives a patch to wear on their Pathfinder sash. Usually the presentation occurs during a ceremony that takes place at an investiture service. *Adventist Youth Classwork* is an educational program in which Pathfinders achieve basic levels of competency in a sequential fashion. Beginning in fifth grade, youth must complete a list of requirements in the areas of personal growth, spiritual discovery, serving others, health and fitness, youth organization, nature study, outdoor living, and honor enrichment for each level before attaining the next level. Each class reflects a particular grade or age level as outlined below:

Friend — **fifth grade**
Companion — **sixth grade**
Explorer — **seventh grade**
Ranger — **eighth grade**
Voyager — **ninth grade**
Guide — **tenth grade**
Master Guide — **eleventh and twelvth grades**

The philosophy behind progressive classwork rests on a number of counsels given by Ellen G. White, one of which states: "As a rule, the exercise most beneficial to the youth will be found in useful employment. The little child finds both diversion and development in play; and his sports should be such as to promote not only physical, but mental and spiritual growth. As he gains strength and intelligence, the best recreation will be found in some line of effort that is useful. That which trains the hand to helpfulness, and teaches the young to bear their share of life's burdens, is most effective in promoting the growth of mind and character" (*Education*, p. 215).

CHAPTER FOUR

IN KINDNESS, TRUTH, AND PURITY

1970s

By 1970 the church had 58,371 Pathfinders and 2,768 clubs. During this decade Norm Middag, MV secretary of the Florida Conference, put together the first conference Pathfinder council, a concept that the Florida Conference still operates under.

Middag also helped launch the Yes (Youth Emergency Services) program in the Southern Union Conference. A community services corp designed to involve Adventist young people in both disaster relief and general community service, it would attract many Pathfinders. It began when Hurricane Camille smashed into Gulfport and Biloxi, Mississippi, on August 17, 1969, killing 300 and causing millions of dollars of devastation. The official Adventist relief vans distributed clothing and bedding. But they were not alone.

A group of Adventist young people also went to help. Borrowing a small van, they first began bringing fresh water to those cleaning up debris and making emergency property repairs. Next they brought bedding and supplies to wherever they found storm victims. Then they helped clear streets and assist in cleanup work.

From their experience evolved YES. With the approval of the Southern Union and the Florida Conference and the cooperation of area senior academies, Adventist Youth in Action (AYA) centers, and a number of supporting churches, Middag organized four YES units. The conference had north, central, and south units, with an additional unit at the Forest Lake Seventh-day Adventist Church.

Each YES chapter had a local director, a youth captain, and a van. The vans were obtained from a bakery company that went out of business, and were painted and stocked with emergency tools and supplies. The young people wore an official work uniform of blue coveralls and hard hats. The dress uniform consisted of a blue shirt with a black tie and dark blue pants or skirt. Each uniform displayed a red and white YES insignia.

To be a member of a YES unit the young person had to be a junior in high school or at least 16 years of age. He or she had to have parental permission, a recommendation from a church, school, or other institution, and a dri-ver's license. Besides obtaining a uniform, members had to participate in at least one operation a month.

The chapters met an hour and a half each week to study disaster-control procedures. The classes might deal with vehicle traffic control, first-aid certification, special procedures for handling dead bodies, wreckage cleanup techniques, and the proper use of emergency tools and equipment. Each member had to be able to handle extension ladders, fire extinguishers, power chain saws, axes, emergency gas lights, electric generators, water purification apparatus, and communication devices such as scanners and two-way radios.

The Southern Union 1979 camporee took place near the home town of U.S. president Jimmy Carter.

The groups did not restrict themselves just to disasters and other emergencies, though they did help out when a tornado struck the Capistrano Apartments in Altamonte Springs, Florida. In December 1970 a YES group of 16 traveled 150 miles from Orlando to the Lake City, Florida, church and painted it both inside and out in a single day.

When freezing weather destroyed much of the Florida vegetable crop, an Orlando radio station suggested placing trucks around the city to collect food for the jobless migrant workers. The local YES group volunteered their truck. YES teams also helped the elderly clean their yards and houses, trim hedges, wash windows, and do other chores and errands. They gathered food at Thanksgiving and provided traffic control at accidents in cooperation with the sheriff's office and highway patrol.

First Pathfinder Camporee in Brazil

November 14-16, 1975, 14 years after the first Pathfinder Club organized in Riberao, Preto, in the state of São Paulo, Brazil, 300 eager Pathfinders (Desvravadores) and 200 directors, guests, and family members gathered in the Rio Grande Conference in Campestre Novo, Rio Grande do Sul, for the first conference camporee ever held in the country. Jose Maria Barbosa da Silva, then youth director of the Rio Grande Conference, and Jason McCracken, the first African-American student missionary to Brazil, spearheaded the event. Also in attendance was Rodolfo Gorski, then youth director of the South Brazil Conference. Jose Maria authorized McCracken, his associate youth director and Pathfinder specialist, to plan the camporee. Some clubs traveled more than 400 miles to attend. The highlight of the gathering was a church service in a cave that opened on to the campsite.

The Silver Anniversary of Pathfindering, launched in 1974 and extending throuhout 1975, selected the slogan "Smile; You're a Pathfinder." Lowell Litten, editor of *Guide* magazine at the time, wrote the words and music for the accompanying theme song by the same title.

Also, as part of the celebration, "Explore 74" served as the selected camporee theme as Pathfinders explored the life of Jesus Christ, the greatest Explorer of all. Pathfinders sold 5,000 specially made souvenir plates to help promote their organization. The ultimate goal of this celebration was to encourage youth and adults to get involved in the ministry of Pathfindering and to launch many new Pathfinder clubs around the world. The enthusiasm obviously caught on, as the number of Pathfinders around the world nearly doubled from a membership of 85,191 to 161,402 members in 7,203 clubs by 1980. The twenty-fifth anniversary celebration, according to Leo Ranzolin, former world Pathfinder director, was responsible for "putting Pathfindering on the map overseas."

Italian Union of Churches. The Italian counterpart to Pathfinders, called Explo, comes from the word "explorer." It began in 1970 thanks to Pastor Hugo Visani, youth director of the Italian Conference at that time. However, Adventist young people in Italy had been gathering for activities similar to those of Pathfinder clubs since 1945.

During the 1970s Pathfindering continued to grow and spread around the world and meet new needs and interests. In 1970 John H. Hancock became world youth director, and Leo Ranzolin assumed the position of world Pathfinder director. A revision of the MV handbook, new honors such as model rocketry and rock climbing were added, and the Pioneer class was renamed Ranger.

The next year a division camporee gathered in Vasterang, Sweden, and Jan S. Doward made the first Pathfinder movie. Doward filmed Gary Rust's club in the Chesapeake Conference as it went through drill practice. Pioneer youth leader C. Lester Bond died in April 1971.

The year 1972 celebrated the fifieth anniversary of the JMV classes. The Euro-Africa Division held a camporee July 19-29 in Villach, Austria. New honors included ecology and copper enameling. Harriet Maxsom Holt died in March.

A revised Pathfinder staff manual came off the press in 1974, and the Australasian Division held a camporee January 1-6, 1975, at Yarramundi, Sydney. The thirtieth Pathfinder anniversary celebration began in 1976, and new honors included advanced cycling, dog care and training, quilting, tunbling and balancing, and wilderness leadership.

Jan Doward produced the second Pathfinder film, **Pathfinder Club Meeting**. The Euro-Africa Division held a camporee July 11-19, 1977, in Italy, and the Northern Europe-West Africa Division convened at Kallioniemen, Finland, July 19-25. A division-wide camporee assembled at Bangalore, India, November 4-8, 1978. In 1979 the church changed the name Missionary Volunteers to Adventist Youth. Junior Missionary Volunteers became Adventist Junior Youth, and Pre-ADY became Adventurers (for grades 1-4). The Church Heritage Manual was revised.

CHAPTER FIVE

A MESSAGE TO TELL THE WORLD

1980s

In 1983 a new magazine called *Pathfinder* began publication in North America. Geared to Pathfinders and their leaders, it featured adventure stories, mission highlights, crafts and activity ideas, puzzles, Pathfinder news, and a host of other topics designed to involve youth in wholesome Christian activity.

World Club Feature: Conquistadores do Rei

In March 1987 Master Guide Henrique Carlos Carolino founded the Conquistadores do Rei Pathfinder Club of Ceará, Brazil. Under the current direction of Ana Cristina dos Santos, the 35-member club has participated in four regional camporees and is classified as a maxim, or level A club. The

Latvia Pathfinders

Conquistadores' uniform and flag both are a bold yellow and black. The youth enjoy outdoor activities such as camping, hiking, and mountain climbing, and have participated in at least 40 camping trips. Other activities include survival camping, honors, Bible classes, missionary and educational activities, and sports.

The February 24, 1983, *Adventist Review* printed this report written by World Pathfinder Director Mike Stevenson: "More than 4,000 Pathfinders from 170 clubs attended the bi-union Brisbane River [Australia] Camporee, January 4-9. This was the largest overseas camporee in the 33-year history of Pathfindering.

"Clubs attending came from as far away as Perth, in Western Australia, as well as from parts of New Zealand. Because the Government of Papua New Guinea is interested in the Pathfinder Club as a means of educating children, the Papua new Guinea Union Mission sent all of its youth directors to participate in this historic event. . . . Citing statistics related to the dramatic number of midteenagers involved in crime, [the South Queensland acting police commissioner] suggested that being a Pathfinder is one of the best crime-prevention programs in his area of jurisdiction.

"The entire camporee was centered around the book of Acts. The streets of the camp were named according to places in the book. Delegates areas were named as in Roman times. There were centurions and other officers as mentioned in the book of Acts. The young people captured the idea of life in those days and went away with a better understanding of this important book."

Inter-America

Nearly 4,000 Pathfinders participated in the Pathfinders to Heaven Camporee of the Inter-American Division, held March 24-30, 1983. Young people from 28 countries of IAD attended the camporee, held at the Oaxtepec Resort, south of Oaxtepec, Mexico. The July 14, 1983, issue of the *Adventist Review* reports that "some of the young people had traveled through troubled areas of Central America to attend, but border incidents only delayed rather than prevented their coming. . . .

Inter-American camporee

Several hundred Pathfinders were disappointed when travel arrangements became impossible. A devaluation of the local currency just before their departure caused an enormous increase in travel costs, and they had no time to make up the difference."

Energies and excitement ran high as the ceremony opened with the various contingents waving their national flags and marching in step with the tunes played by the Montemorelos University band. One memorable highlight during the Pathfinder Bible contest occurred when junior Pathfinder Freddie McNiel, whose family was serving as missionaries in Honduras,

expertly answered round after round of questions without error. he inspired fellow Pathfinders and leaders alike to study more and memorize the Word of God.

Camp Hale Camporee

Fifteen thousand youth and adults converged at Camp Hale, July 31 to August 6, 1985, near Leadville, Colorado, in the Rocky Mountains to attend the first North American Division camporee. A daily newspaper, an FM radio station, police force, post office, bank, bus system, fire department, five miles of water lines, a sewage system, stores, pay

The camporee wove everything around the concept Adventures in Service, with each evening program following a variation of that theme. The different state conference youth directors planned the various evening, Sabbath morning, and Sunday afternoon programs.

Pathfinders had the privilege of interviewing various celebrities, including prominent Black leader Jesse Jackson, Skylab astronaut William Pogue, Steve Pennington, and two young actors from the Bill Cosby TV show. Olympic gold medalist Jeff Blatnik related his experience winning in Greco-Roman wrestling the previous year. He brought the Olympic torch to the stage Monday night for a candlelight service led by Bob Holbrook, then youth director of the Illinois Conference.

The young people would long remember the show Victor the Wrestling Bear put on

telephones, and thousands of temporary residents made this settlement a virtual city.

Three years of planning and preparation created a rich and memorable seven-day event of camping, hiking, canoeing, rafting, rock climbing, obstacle courses, gondola rides, and other recreational activities. It was also an educational extravaganza that included such exhibits as an Old Testament sanctuary; theme trails featuring handicap awareness, conservation, and Pathfinder history; a wilderness camp and a mining camp; honor booths; and more—all to foster in the Pathfinders a great love and appreciation for their church and a desire to serve their Saviour.

Obstacle courses have been popular at all camporees.

Camp Hale was constant and exciting activity.

Sunday afternoon. The 23-year-old Canadian brown bear weighed in at 650 pounds and stood eight feet three inches tall. His trainer, George, demonstrated bear wrestling, then offered anyone in the audience a chance to volunteer to wrestle the bear. Egged on by George, the Pathfinders began to chant, "We want Mike! We want Mike!" Mike Stevenson, then world Pathfinder leader, entered the cage and received a bear hug and kiss.

The stage in the main assembly area rested on top of six flatbed truck trailers. So the large audience could see what was happening on the stage even at a distance, television cameras projected the scene on a giant 33-ton Diamond Vision screen. The 1984 Los Angeles Olympics had used one of the screens. BiFrost Technical Effects from North Hollywood, California, provided a popular laser show. On Sabbath afternoon and each evening the Pathfinders launched thousands of helium-filled balloons. Each had a slip of paper attached, offering a reward to the finders if they put their names and addresses on the forms and mailed them back. By mid-September 60 tags had come from seven states.

Jeff Wood wrote a special song for the camporee telling the Pathfinders that "we are His hands . . . His feet . . . His light . . . His love." The Pathfinders had the chance to put this theme into practice through special ministry. More than 1,400 young people signed up to perform a special service in the surrounding communities. Some traveled from five to 60 miles to their service location.

Bill Little, owner of the Little Cliff's Bakery in Aspen, Colorado, and his crew baked what was then the world's largest cake. The 4,261.44 - pound cake was 505 feet and three and three-fourth inches long and 18 feet wide. The center section was eight feet tall. Sunday morning a truck and semitrailer brought the cake to the camp.

Fifty Pathfinders were baptized at Camp Hale, and another 100 requested baptism after the event.

More than 100 Maranatha Flights International people helped build, maintain, and then tear down the camporee facilities.

Similar division-wide camporees had occured in Northern Europe in 1971, in Euro-Africa in 1972, in the South Pacific Division in 1975, in Southern Asia in 1978, in Inter-America in 1983, and in South America in 1984.

Africa

Daniel Davis, Adventist youth director in the Africa-Indian Ocean Division, watched the growth of Pathfindering there. In Ghana and Nigeria the uniformed Pathfinders paraded with a distinctive British marching style. Baraka Muganda (later world Adventist Youth leader) presided over the first Africa youth congress, held in Nairobi, Kenya, in 1986. Kenya Pathfinders formed a honor guard to welcome the nation's president, D. Arab Moi. The country's Pathfinders also had a unique style of witnessing by telling Bible stories using picture rolls.

The French Swiss Conference

Pathfinders in the French-speaking part of Switzerland celebrated their 50-year anniversary March 4, 5, 1989, in Renens and Gland. A Lausanne youth club officially organized in 1939 under the leadership of Madeleine Favre, Clairmonde Hoffman, and Sylvain Meyer. The club went by the name Youth Missionary Volunteers. Today the French Swiss Conference has 13 organized Pathfinder clubs with more than 200 members.

Largest Union Camporee Held in Brazil

In 1986 Jose Maria Barbosa da Silva, youth director of the recently organized Central Brazil Union and the South American Division, held, in the city of Avare, São Paulo, Brazil, what was then the largest union Pathfinder Camporee in the nation. At the request of the mayor of Avare more than 2,000 Pathfinders convened at a city-owned camping facility. Clubs came from as far as 2,500 kilometers away. One Pathfinder group arrived on a flatbed truck. It later placed among the top ten clubs.

The event also marked the first time that Pathfinder leaders used computers to evaluate each club on outreach ministry, AY honors, discipline, baptisms, and so forth. As each club reported, leaders entered the data into an Apple II computer. A special program rated the club. Using a special code, the clubs could have the computer print a copy of their activities for the current year.

The evaluations rewarded clubs with strong programs in their churches and communities. To eliminate competitiveness, instead of ranking the clubs as first, second, or third, the leaders rewarded a club no matter how small by whether it met certain criteria.

The highlight of the camporee was its opening exercises. The local mayor and government officials sat on a professional stage with thousands of colored lights. Video cameras showed the program on television projection screens. Fireworks accompanied a visual presentation of the second coming of Christ.

Pathfinders and staff purchased newly designed Pathfinder gear at a special mall set up at the campsite. A candlelight ceremony dur-

ing which Pathfinder directors lit more than 2,000 candles symbolized the young people's commitment to be lights in their communities. It also reinforced the *"Ele Esta au Leme"* (He Is at the Helm) camporee theme.

In 1988, 17 Pathfinders from the Florida Conference didn't just make history, they helped to recreate it. At the William Miller farm in Low Hampton, New York, the Florida Pathfinders worked to restore the historic site to its original beauty by rebuilding walls, clearing paths, and making trails. They returned two more times to continue their work. Many clubs have since participated in this unique restoration project in which they built not only walls but their spiritual lives as well.

Pathfinders and Mission Service

Short-term mission trips give Pathfinders a taste of mission service. One example is the Michigan Conference Teen Mission Impact program. It was started by Merill Fleming in 1981, and it continued under his successor, Terry Dodge. The program takes 25 teen Pathfinders and pairs of doctors, dentists, optometrists, and other support staff to the Dominican Republic for two weeks each year. The group conduct clinics for eight or nine days in different towns, helping 3,000-4,000 people. The Pathfinders and medical

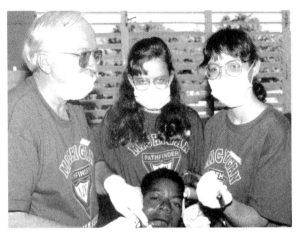

Hands-on experience helping to pull teeth

teams bring medical and dental supplies as well as used eyeglasses to use in the various clinics.

The Michigan Conference sees several benefits from conducting such a program:

1. It gives the teens an opportunity to see another culture.

2. The Pathfinders have hands-on experience in the medical, dental, and optical clinics. They give shots, pull teeth, and help fit glasses.

3. Some of the young people become student missionaries during college.

4. The experience has encouraged some to enter health-related careers.

5. An evangelistic series follows each clinic. Churches later organize in the towns the young people visit.

"My trip to the Dominican Republic was an unbelievable experience," Bridget McCarthy said after her project. "I would highly recommend it to anyone with a caring nature and the desire to help others. I began it not knowing what I was getting into, and left with a whole new perspective to life. I have always known that I was blessed with good health, loving family and friends, and countless opportunities. But it wasn't until I had experienced life in the Dominican Republic that I understood the reality of a developing country where people are not healthy and do not have access to medicine and health care. Also, I discovered how many more opportunities children have in the U.S.

Dominican Republic mission trip—lineup for the health-care clinic

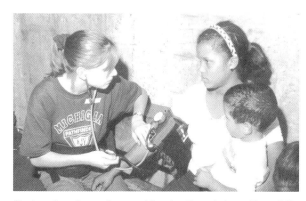

Caring for those in need in the Dominican Republic

"The children who were lucky enough to attend our clinics had no shoes and were in poor health, but they were as happy as could be and were grateful for the vitamins, medicine, toothbrushes, eyeglasses, and services we were able to provide. Their faces would light up when we gave them a toy after they completed their exams. It gave myself and the other volunteers a wonderful sense of fulfillment. No matter how bad the conditions were (weather, traveling long distances, bathrooms, lack of cleanliness, and lack of sleep), when we left a clinic it felt as if we were on top of the world. I personally felt that there was nothing in the world I could not accomplish. It was the most amazing feeling."

Fortieth Anniversary

The celebration of the fortieth anniversary of Pathfindering took place from 1986 to 1989 as Pathfinders around North America held camporees and events to commemorate this historic milestone. The Gulf States Conference featured pioneer Pathfinder John Hancock, who thrilled spellbound youth with stories of the past.

Another highlight of the fortieth anniversary occurred when the Columbia Union Conference hosted the Friendship Camporee in Pennsylvania, led by Ron Stretter. Clubs from all over North America and some international guests participated in the five-day event referred to as a "spiritual feast." On Sabbath afternoon 156 young people were baptized.

Fortieth anniversary pin

Again space permits us to look at only a few examples of what was going on among Pathfinder clubs. The following clubs only hint at the vibrancy of Pathfindering.

Loma Linda Korean Pathfinders

The Korean Pathfinder Club, established in 1987 holds a steady membership of 18 to 24 members and has had the same director, Byron Hazley, for all but three years of its existence. They adopted as their mascot the Korean tiger. Their first Pathfinder Fair included a person in a tiger suit who marched with the group. This event paralleled the 1988 Seoul Olympics for which the mascot was also a tiger. The club placed first in its conference during its first year as a functioning club.

We've highlighted here many of the positive aspects of Pathfindering, but all clubs have their challenges. When asked to share some of the difficulties of maintaining a functioning club, Byron Hazley gave this reality check:

"One of the challenges is keeping the interest level as each person gets older. As with most churches, the high school group tends to get forgotten. If we can retain more students as teens through high school, we can plug into the vast resources and activities of the conference T [teen counselor] program. Last year we had two T's. This year we have five."

Another challenge Byron described involved maintaining good counselors. The cultural and language differences between American-raised, English-speaking Koreans and immigrant Koreans needed to be met. A mixed staff, comprised mostly of parents with kids in the club, seems to be a positive formula.

"Our staff's purpose is to instill Christian values and a sense of mission in each of our kids through our total program," Byron comments. "Our goal is to make each of them feel it is a privilege to be in Pathfinders and to maintain a Christian lifestyle at any age."

La Vida Mission Pathfinders

The La Vida Mission Thunderbirds renewed their mission in the late 1980s "to give Navajo youth a sense of culture through nature, crafts, and other activities, and above all, [an understanding of] God's purpose for all of us."

This Navajo club maintains an average of 10 to 15 members. The club lasted first for about three years, dying out in the mid-1980s. Jim and Vicky Spicer, aided by the present Pathfinder director, Bob Blair, revived it around 1988 or 1989. They felt that La Vida needed a Pathfinder Club to augment its boarding school program.

The club maintained its vitality through the early- to mid-1990s. It then faced the challenge of maintaining the students' focus and providing enough adult involvement. Strong leadership has helped the club to survive.

Like most Pathfinder clubs, the Thunderbirds enjoy drilling and marching. These skills, along with their camping abilities, help the club to shine at many Pathfinder fairs. They often take first place in the making of pine derby cars at Pathfinder fairs.

Loma Linda Chinese Church Pathfinders

Pathfinders of the Loma Linda Chinese church in California share the same goals as other Pathfinder clubs around the world: to bring its members "closer to God and to prepare them to be better Christians." Also, like other Pathfinder groups, they have an intensive outreach program in their community that includes canned food drives and nursing home ministries. According to its director, Gordon Chan, the club members have become very close during recent years. "A situation that helped us to grow was when a group of members decided to leave our church and start their own Pathfinders, which left us with no one to lead our group. The kids really wanted the club to continue, so I accepted the challenge to help them," Chan said.

The majority of the club's members are musically gifted and play a variety of instruments. It has enhanced their marching and drilling techniques.

CHAPTER SIX

A TRUTH THAT WILL SET US FREE

1990s

January 1, 1991, stands out as a significant date in Pathfinder history. Under the direction of Norm Middag, then North American Division Pathfinder director, Pathfinders rode the first Seventh-day Adventist float entered in the Pasadena Tournament of Roses Parade, the most widely observed public celebration of its kind in North America. During December 1990 Pathfinders from all across North America had helped decorate the Adventist float, entitled "Playing in Peace." It depicted children of varying ethnic and cultural groups playing together. The float employed only natural materials, such as poinsettias, carnations, rose petals, cinnamon, cornmeal, walnuts, and almonds, and represented the 190 countries that have an Adventist presence.

Making of the float "Playing in Peace"

The Tournament of Roses Parade was the largest public relations event that the Seventh-day Adventist Church ever participated in. An estimated 1 million people viewed the event live, and another 400 million in 80 nations and territories around the world watched a later re-broadcast. Referred to as Witness Through Roses, the outreach provided numerous opportunities for Adventist youth to share their faith, not only by participating in the parade, but through media interviews, speaking engagements, literature distribution, and community service outreach projects in conjunction with the Tournament of Roses Parade events.

The Witness Through Roses project continued for three years in a row. During its first year of participation, the Adventist float, "Playing in Peace," won the Lathrop K. Leishman Trophy, an award bestowed on the

most beautiful entry from a non-commercial sponsor. In 1992 the Adventist float, having the theme "Discovering the World of Service," won the National Award Trophy for the best use of roses. Although the 1993 float, "Enjoying and Caring for Nature," did not win an award, the impact of the Adventist witness was even greater than in previous years. "The first year 400 million people heard the name Seventh-day Adventist. By 1993 the number of people who heard the name Seventh-day Adventist had grown to more

Pathfinders on the Rose Bowl Parade floats

than 1 billion," says Norm Middag.

In addition, under the leadership of Arnold and Dixie Plata, the North American Division Pathfinders decorated a non-Adventist float each year from 1992 to 1998. Each float that they worked on won an award. Pathfinders became known in the float industry as detailed decorators.

"The supervisor of the float decoration company, Darrell Bender, told me," Dixie recalls, "that 'a float had never been decorated without everyone working every day from Christmas to New Years. It just couldn't be done.' Of course he had never worked with Pathfinder people before.

"When Norm Middag made arrangements for the Pathfinders to decorate the float, he told the company, Fiesta Parade Floats, that as Seventh-day Adventists we would not do anything on the float on Saturdays. The company was reluctant to deal with a church group anyway—they had had problems with religious groups in the past. Now they were sure that we would not finish in time.

"A total of 563 Pathfinders and adults, ranging in age from 8 to 88, worked two to 20 eight-hour shifts. On the Friday afternoon before the parade we cleaned up our area and sent the decorators home early so they could avoid the heavy Friday afternoon traffic. On Sabbath, Bender and a few of his friends and family visited the float to see what still needed

Norm Middag, John Hancock, and Lawrence Paulson at Dare to Care Camporee

finders came from the United States, Canada, Australia, Bermuda, Brazil, Estonia, Guam, Guatemala, Hong Kong, Iceland, Paraguay, the Philippines, Russia, South Africa, Sweden, and Ukraine. "Many more wanted to come, but we were limited by the camping capacity at Bandimere and by the seating available at Red Rocks," said Ron Whitehead, who directed the event. "Registrations sold out nearly five months ahead of the event. To my knowledge, this had never happened before with an Adventist event in North America."

Although the Bandimere Speedway was one and a half miles long and provided 100,000 square feet of tent space, it was just too small for all those who wanted to come. The evening programs took place at the Red Rocks Amphitheater five miles away. It took 75 busses one and a half hours to shuttle everyone there.

to be done. To his astonishment he discovered that we were a day and a half ahead of schedule and would be done on time for the parade.

"After sundown Saturday more than 100 people showed up to finish the float. Several hours before the deadline we cleaned up our work area, and several volunteered to help complete other floats. Besides the honor of winning an award, the Pathfinders and decoration crew established a positive relationship with the float company. The company began telling us how much they enjoyed working with us."

In 1992 preparations began for the Dare to Care International Camporee held at the Bandimere Speedway in Morrison, Colorado, August 2-6, 1994. Twelve thousand Path-

The Dare to Care flag flying high over the camporee

A portion of the crowd at the Dare to Care Camporee in Bandimere, Colorado

Through a variety of musical and dramatic evening programs centering on the "Dare to Care" theme, the camporee led Pathfinders to develop a closer relationship with Christ. Friday's evening program, "The Centurion's Story," portrayed through musical drama Christ's death and resurrection. When Jesus came forth from the tomb, the audience burst into applause. The play made it real to them that Jesus was alive and would return. The main evening speaker was LeCalire Litchfield from Collegedale, Tennessee. Loving to share Jesus with others, he told the Pathfinders, "We are a people who must fall deeply in love with Jesus day by day. In doing so, we will joyfully enter into His rest every waking moment of our lives."

Daytime activities included kite flying, a

healthy choices tent, an obstacle course, a handicap awareness tent, drill teams, horseback riding, hot-air balloon rides, daily drag races, archery, waterskiing, canoeing, kayaking, and the Pathfinder Heritage Display. For three days 3,000 Pathfinders participated in clothing and food drives, graffiti cleanup, building for Habitat for Humanity, and an anti-drug march in downtown Denver. On Wednesday many Pathfinders participated in making a mile-long string of shrink-wrapped vegetarian hot dogs that snaked back and forth on the bleachers. It took 2,200 pounds of wheat and 350 pounds of water to make the 10,000 Natural touch brand hotdogs in the string.

On Sabbath, the final day of the camporee, 29 Pathfinders were baptized and hundreds planned for baptism in the near future.

The special guest one evening was Lawrence Paulson, then 93. He told the young people how much his religious faith had spurred him to help develop the Pathfinder program. "My faith means everything," he explained. "That's the reason I've been involved with Pathfinders. We are trying to train Pathfinders to be real Christian boys and girls and fine men and women."

Another guest was Josh Gomez of Denver, who was honored twice as Pathfinder of the year. When he was 8 months of age his parents learned that he had hemophilia. His blood did not clot properly, and he bruised easily. Because he bled so easily, he had to have many blood transfusions. In 1990 Josh learned that a transfusion had infected him with AIDS.

Despite his shock and anger at what had happened to him, Josh decided to give back to his community some of the love and support that it had offered him. He learned about a two-day 150-mile bike race to raise funds for a multiple sclerosis project. Although his parents objected, he felt that he should enter it. Although he needed only $150 to participate, he collected $550. For three months he practiced riding 10 miles each day. On the day of the race his father rode with him. Even though Josh had to walk his bike up the long hills and his legs ached, he kept going, covering 86 miles the first day and 55 the next. To honor his Pathfinder spirit, the church chose Josh as one of those who rode on the Pathfinder float in the 1992 Tournament of Roses Parade in California.

The Pathfinder Heritage Museum, under the direction of Arnold and Dixie Plata, Pathfinder historians, was a big hit. The Platas developed the Pathfinder Heritage Display. Dixie has been involved with JMV, MV, and the Pathfinder program since 1946. In 1950 she participated in a "first" club in the Upper Columbia Conference at Spangle, Washington. From there she moved to Southeastern

The Pathfinder Heritage Museum preserves artifacts of Pathfiner history.

California Conference, where she worked in the Loma Linda Pathfinder Club in various capacities, including craft instructor and counselor. During the 1970s she served as club secretary and then director of the Loma Linda, California, Pathfinder Club. The local Dorcas Society passed along through her some Pathfinder materials. The uniform pieces she shared with Pathfinders who needed them. The others she stored for later use.

The museum, depicting the history of youth work in the Seventh-day Adventist Church through MV, JMV, and Pathfinders, was housed in a 7,200-square-foot tent. Displays of various historical events gave Seventh-day Adventist youth many fun learned opportunities. It was the beginning of what would become a valuable collection of Pathfinder memorabilia. Dixie's

husband, Arnold Plata, began to collect JMV and MV manuals and certificates. She gathered uniform emblems and various Pathfinder, MF, and JMV memorabilia.

By 1980 Arnold was building display cases and Dixie was putting together attractive displays to share the history of the Pathfinder Club. They presented the displays first at local churches in the Southeastern California Conference for investiture ceremonies and Pathfinder Day celebrations. During the next five years they added many more items, including stories from such pioneers as C. Lester Bond, Eldine W. Dunbar, Henry T. Bergh,

Pathfinders pose with a photo of the Tournament of Roses parade pathfinder float.

Theodore E. Lucas, John H. Hancock, Laurence Skinner, Lawrence Paulson, and Harry Garlick. The Platas deeply appreciate the generosity of the many dedicated world division and union Pathfinder directors who have helped the Youth Museum collection grow by sharing their stories and memorabilia of the history of youth in the Seventh-day Adventist Church from 1879 to the present.

After Camp Hale in 1985, their collection seemed to mushroom. It was at that time that they began to travel and display the collection at Pathfinder leadership conventions, youth camps, fairs, camporees, and camp meetings throughout the North American Division. The couple also worked with Advent Village in Battle Creek, Michigan, to help with displays there that depict the importance of youth ministry around the world. Their goal is to enable the youth of the church to realize, understand, and appreciate past history; get involved in their local churches; and plan for a future in God's kingdom.

John Hancock, former world youth leader, and Lawrence Paulson, Mr. Pathfinder, were the featured guests of the Pathfinder History Museum at the Dare to Care Camporee. Talking with former Pathfinders and meeting new ones, they shared Pathfinder stories and signed autographs.

Also in 1994, the North American Division created a Teen Leadership Training (TLT) program for teen Pathfinders, an adaptation of the FLITE (Future Leaders in Training Excellence) program developed by Sligo, Maryland, Pathfinder leaders Franklin Moses and Darlene and Glen Milam. The TLT program mentors Pathfinders who want to advance to more challenging levels of leadership and service. The division established the program in order to have one recognized program for teen training throughout its territory.

Glen Milam tells the story of its development: "As club leaders, we had been looking for a way to challenge our teens. Many of our teens stated clearly that they were not interested in being counselors. They wanted to work with the club, but in other aspects of club operation and outreach. While returning from an outing, Franklin, Darlene, and I put together the basic outline. Our premise was: if we wanted to teach someone to run a club, how would we organize the roles? Franklin, a teen at the time, then wrote up a list of tasks. Darlene and I enlarged and refined his lists. Franklin served as the FLITE director, and had up to a dozen FLITE officers under his command."

On September 9, 1995, the Southeastern California Conference kicked off the Pathfinder Golden Jubilee celebration in recognition of 50 years of Pathfindering in the conference. The event took place at the La

Sierra Pavilion. The next May a Pathfinder parade and fair ended the year-long celebration. Throughout North America other clubs hosted similar events between 1996 and 1999. The Southern California Conference held a Fiftieth Anniversary Camporee September 5-8 at the Santa Fe Dam Recreation Park in Irwindale. The camporee had 1,096 registered Pathfinders. The series of fiftieth anniversary celebrations culminated with the Discover the Power International Camporee in August of 1999 at Oshkosh, Wisconsin.

Master Guide camporee in Chile

On June 19, 1996, Marcus Giddings, a member of the Beltsville, Maryland, Bronco Pathfinder Club, was one of 22 Seventh-day Adventists and 5,500 "community heroes" who participated in passing the Olympic flame from torch to torch across the United States. Marcus' work among the homeless in Washington, D.C., earned him the title of community hero. In all, 10,000 people helped carry the flame more than 15,000 miles through 42 states and 29 state capitals. Two days after carrying the flame, Marcus also had the privilege of meeting and shaking hands with President Bill Clinton at a special White House ceremony.

During January 1998 the South American Division held the first Master Guide camporee in Chile with more than 1,000 pathfinder leaders attending.

Pathfinders in South America are very active on both local and national levels. The divisions' major outreach emphasis, known as "Supermissão" (Supermission), is a program in which Pathfinders evangelize the community through donating blood, building homes, visiting hospitals and orphanages, planting trees, distributing pamphlets, and presenting health awareness programs. In addition to these local ministries, each year the young people participate in an anniversary parade during which hundreds of clubs appear on national television, complete with Pathfinder drills.

Brazil alone is about the same size as Australia or the United States, with a population of 145 million. It is no wonder that South American Pathfinders are experiencing as much as 50 percent growth each year.

On February 12-14, 1998, the first North

American Division Master Guide Convention assembled in Los Angeles, California, under the direction of Willie Oliver, NAD director of Pathfinder Ministries. A commemoration of 70 years of the Master Guide program, and one of a series of events in honor of 50 years of Pathfindering, the event allowed more than 500 Master Guides from more than 20 countries to gain certification in such areas as outdoor skills, church heritage, and youth evangelism. At the convention, which invested 24 Master Guides, Oliver shared the following observations on the Master Guide program: "People who enjoy working with young people are drawn to this program because it provides them with leadership tools and training. Since churches across the division are always in need of trained ministry leaders, Master Guides are ready to fill important positions and do their part to hasten the coming of Jesus Christ." Indeed, that's what Pathfindering is all about.

Pathfinders Around the World; World Pathfinder Directors

A movement is only as great as its leaders, and the organization of Pathfinders is no exception. The Seventh-day Adventist Church has had in the history of Pathfindering many such talented, spiritual individuals, filled with zeal for the salvation of youth, to lead the program.

Willie Oliver speaks at seventieth anniversary Master Guide convention

God has especially ignited the Pathfinder ministry through the talents and fortitude of dedicated individuals:

Laurence A. Skinner (1950-1963)
John H. Hancock (1964-1970)
Leo Ranzolin (1970-1980)
Mike Stevenson (1980-1986)
**   (Mike Stevenson died in 1993)**
Malcolm Allen (1986-1995)
Baraka G. Muganda (1995-1997)
Robert Holbrook (1997 to present)

John Hancock retired after 41 years of service; Malcolm Allen became a conference administrator in Australia; Leo Ranzolin became a general vice president of the General

Conference; and Laurence A. Skinner retired in 1972 after 51 years of service. Current World Pathfinder director Robert Holbrook assumed the challenge of carrying Pathfindering into the new millennium.

Many of these leaders had mentors when they were young. Robert Holbrook entered his first Pathfinder training course at the age of 15 after hearing Bob Tyson, Nebraska Conference youth director, say, "If you want to work with kids, you have to be an outdoors person." Holbrook enjoyed working with other young people, so he became involved in every outdoor activity imaginable, including caving, mountain climbing, distance cycling, and canoeing. He is even listed in a recent *Who's Who of American Birders*. After introducing caving to South American Pathfinders, he started the Adventist caving club Cadesbra, a coined word that means "Brazilian Pathfinder cave" in Portuguese.

Each previous world director influenced this future Pathfinder leader in one way or another. Holbrook remembers specific impressions they made:

"John Hancock was one of the most productive leaders I ever encountered. He got tons of Pathfinder materials into print. The thing I remember most about him, and what he is best known for, is his accordion. John took that accordion with him all around the world. He had it with him when he visited us down on the Amazon, and he always had a new song to teach the kids.

"Another thing that impressed me was how John Hancock could pick up just enough words in most of the major languages to communicate with people wherever he went in the world. People appreciated him because of his willingness to be one of them.

"Leo Ranzolin has always been 'just Leo.' He never changes no matter what the situation. Ranzolin responds personally to every question and acknowledges every letter and comment. Leo speaks, acts, and lives on the same level as his fellow workers.

"Malcolm Allen didn't mind roughing it. He could sleep on a board, a table, the floor—you name it—as readily as a bed. Allen was very accommodating to every culture he encountered, and to Pathfinders. Whatever the Pathfinders ate, he ate, and claimed that some day he'd write a book on the unusual dishes he's encountered. While in Brazil I traveled with him to six camporees in about four weeks. While there he met with and signed autographs for several thousand Pathfinders and never tired of literally being overrun by them. One of the things that stood out most about Malcolm was that he was very clear in his focus and mission.

"Mike Stevenson was very generous. He

would often send a gift or encouraging card to a fellow colleague in youth ministry, many times having never even met the person. I still recall the wedding gift he gave to me and my wife, Judy. Neither of us knew who the sender was and assumed that it had come from a friend of the other. I had a lot of respect for Mike. You could disagree or debate with him, but that wouldn't change his friendship with you. He never took it personally."

When asked about the future of Pathfinders, Robert Holbrook commented, "I see Pathfinders going all the way to the kingdom. If we don't help kids get there, we need to get out of this business."

North American Division Pathfinder Directors

Les Pitton. For most of its history, Pathfindering in North America had been under the leadership of the General Conference Department of Youth Ministries until 1980 when the North American Division appointed its first youth leader. Les Pitton, an innovative and energetic leader, wasn't daunted by the challenge of charting new waters. Looking back on those pioneering days, he recalls a few highlights of his experience as NAD youth ministries director.

"When I became the North American Division youth director, it was clear that the interest in Pathfindering was waning. For that reason, the union youth leaders and I began a strategic plan to once again build excitement about Pathfindering. It was then that we changed the Pathfinder uniform to be more acceptable to the kids as well as the leaders.

"In 1985 we held the first North American Division Pathfinder camporee. The plan was to make it known to Pathfinders throughout the United States and Canada that Pathfindering was more than a small church club of 10 or 12 kids. We had a hard time getting the leadership to accept the camporee idea, but we got them to agree as long as we didn't ask for a subsidy from the church."

Never getting discouraged, Pitton, along with Norm Middag, Ron Stretter, Dick Duerksen, Chuck Case, and a host of dedicated youth workers, combined their organizational and creative skills to plan Camp Hale, an exciting and spiritual week that all who attended will always remember in a special way. "We wanted to give Pathfindering the excitement that it had in its beginnings and let young people experience one of the largest gatherings in the history of the Seventh-day Adventist Church," Pitton explained.

Another major project launched during Pitton's administration was the *Pathfinder* magazine. "We wanted to get college students involved in youth ministry, and Walla Walla

Les Pitton, Willie Oliver, and Norm Middag

College agreed to take on the project," Pitton explains. For several years the magazine provided an educational resource to enhance the practical skills and to nurture the spiritual growth and development of Pathfinders in North America. The Review and Herald Publishing Association published it for a time under the editorship of Mark Ford.

Les Pitton, who worked with Elsie Russell and Mike Stevenson, set up the North American Pathfinder Distribution Center, known today as Advent Source. "At that time we had to order flags, uniforms, insignia, etc., from [a variety] of vendors, so we decided to set up a distribution center at Union College. We had some challenges at first, such as the sizes being wrong the first time we ordered. But it was a start. Eventually we got the prob-

lems worked out."

Looking into the future, Pitton adds, "Pathfindering is not an option for the church, it's a must. If the church doesn't give more credence to Pathfindering and all of youth ministry, the twenty-first century church will be a miserable failure. No organization, no business, no society can survive without the nurturing of its young. The church is no different. Our only option is to put our money where our mouth is, and that is investing in our youth."

Norm Middag. Norm Middag followed Pitton. Under Middag's leadership, from 1985 to 1996, North American Pathfinder membership grew from 20,000 to 38,000. Fueled by the idea that "Pathfinder adult education provides the experience and opportunity for the Pathfinder ministry to be passed on from one generation to another," Middag made a number of significant contributions to the Pathfinder instructional program during his administration. They include developing adult continuing education curricula for the Master Guide program, the Pathfinder Leadership Award, and the Pathfinder Instructor's Award. Middag also upgraded the Adventist Youth class curriculum during his term of office.

When asked to share the highlights of his administration, Middag talked with enthusiasm about the Witness Through Roses project in which Pathfinders from all over North America collaborated their efforts to enter a float in the annual Rose Bowl Parade. The float was a success and for two years in a row won an award. More important to Middag than the awards earned, however, was the positive public image that the project won for the Seventh-day Adventist Church. "The first year of participation in the parade, 400 million people heard the name Seventh-day Adventist. By 1993 the number of people who heard the name had grown to more than 1 billion. Ellen White said we should get the name in front of the people and that's exactly what this project accomplished."

But creating public awareness of Adventism wasn't the only impact of Witness Through Roses. "This was an event in which adults and youth of the Adventist Church united in one common project. That's a rarity," Middag commented.

What device does Norm Middag offer to future Pathfinder leaders as we enter the twenty-first century? "You are called to be disciples, to go and fulfill the gospel commission. You are commissioned to develop an environment in which young people can form Christlike characters. You are called to leadership for the purpose of influencing youth and adults for citizenship in the new earth. You are to influence human behavior, to make a difference in the communities you serve, and to

be effective leaders for God. A total commitment to your Pathfinder ministry is paramount to reaching the ultimate success."

Willie Oliver. When Norm Middag retired in 1996, Willie Oliver took the helm of NAD Pathfinder ministries. "I've been involved in Pathfinders since I was a boy in a local club myself. As a college student I worked with Pathfinders. Then as a pastor I worked with Pathfinders. And of course, as a conference (Greater New York) and union conference (Atlantic Union) youth director, I worked with Pathfinders. I have always seen Pathfinders as a means to engage children and earliteens in a constructive and instructive Christian curriculum and set of activities to prepare them for service and draw them closer to Jesus."

A skilled leader and Master Guide, Oliver places a high level of importance on training. In keeping with his vision for developing leaders prepared to hasten the second coming of Christ, in February of 1998 Oliver directed the first Master Guide convention held in North America. At this event, delegates from the United States, Canada, Bermuda, and 28 other countries developed their leadership skills to become Master Guides, the highest level of youth training in the denomination.

As the church moves into the twenty-first century, Willie Oliver shares this advice with future Pathfinder leaders: "Make Pathfinders fun, relevant, energetic; not punitive and army-like—it isn't boot camp. If this ministry is to remain relevant in the twenty-first century, it must reach out to the communities in which it operates to touch the lives of the children of non-members as well. The future is more important than the past. Be flexible and willing to change. Without compromising principles, make the form of the ministry always contemporary. Trust God. His power is still available to you."

A Common Bond

Members of a small church in Cameroon in central Africa had little knowledge of Pathfinders. They possessed neither materials nor uniforms, and language barriers raised other problems. The one thing they did have, however, was an eagerness to embrace the world of Pathfindering through the Pathfinder Leadership program.

Miles away, in Harare, Zimbabwe, 1,550 Pathfinders experiencing their first camporee, took a five-mile walk around Lake Kyle, all the while bursting into spontaneous harmony as small groups felt inspired to sing. A short six months prior to the camporee, only 20 percent of the energetic Pathfinders had had uniforms. The clubs now have 80 percent of their members garbed in crisp, new uniforms, cour-

tesy of a local manufacturer (with a little persuasion from former world Pathfinder director Malcolm Allen).

Youth all over the world sing the Pathfinder song as they share the spirit of Pathfindering. Whether they are called Desbravdores in Portuguese-speaking countries, Conquistadore in Spanish-speaking Latin America, Eclaireur in French-speaking countries, Cadets in other parts of Europe, or Pathfinders in the English-speaking world, clubs wave their flags high as they recite the Pathfinder pledge in their native tongues.

Australian Pathfinders continue to be shining lights in their communities. The following appeared in the November 29, 1997, *Record:* "Some 600 Pathfinders from Sydney committed themselves to living drug-free lives by walking across the Harbour Bridge to the Opera House on November 1.

"The highlight of the walk, part of the Greater Sydney Conference Pathfinder Rally, was the release, amid cheers, of 1,500 helium-filled balloons from the steps of the Opera House.

"Speakers at the rally included [former] South Pacific Division youth director Dr. Barry Gane; a Sydney police superintendent Allan Herrmann; Trans-Tasman Union Conference (TTUC) Adventist health director Dr. Terry Butler (who launched the walk); TTUC children's ministries director Carol

McKean; and Wesley Mission Drug-Arm director John O'Hara."

Romania Union Conference

In Romania Pathfindering has a short history. Because of Communism the country had no organized Pathfinder programs for a long time. News about America's Pathfinder program did not reach Romania until 1992, with a visit from world Youth director Malcolm Allen and Euro-Africa Division Youth director Jose Figols. Then Romanian youth leaders nearly exploded with enthusiasm over the prospects of starting a Pathfinder Club in their country. Dana Pridie organized the first club in 1993 at the Lily Church in Bucharest. Under the guidance of Cristian Modan, Romanian Union Pathfinder director, and Ion Buciuman, the union youth director, the newly formed Romanian clubs had 120 members by 1995, 800 by 1995, 2,800 by 1997, and more than 5,000 by 1998. They planned to reach 10,000 by 2000. A team of youth leaders from the Georgia-Cumberland Conference held leadership training seminars and acted as a sister conference.

Another youth director named Szallos Zoltan sent a team of teenagers from Hungary to be trained in a Scout camp (the Hungarian Adventist Pathfinders are also members of the Scout movement). With the help of the trained Scouts, Szallos organized a training camp for Pathfinder leaders in Casa de Piatra. Leon Roman organized another training camp in Busteni that same year.

By the summer of 1995 the country had about 120 Pathfinders in five major cities: Bucharest, Targu Mures, Campina, Ploiesti, and Slobozia. Eighty-three Pathfinders participated in the first summer camp in the Bucegi Mountains.

Pathfinder Clubs of Darmstadt

German Pathfinder history would not be complete without the inclusion of the Pathfinder Clubs of Darmstadt. Darmstadt is a city 18 miles south of Frankfurt. It has about 140,000 inhabitants and only three Seventh-day Adventist churches—Darmstadt-Center (160 members); Darmstadt-Eberstadt (180 members); and Darmstadt-Marienhöhe (more than 600 members). The Pathfinders in all of Darmstadt number more than 300.

The club at Darmstadt-Center has been in existence for nearly 40 years. Formerly known as Jungfreunde-Darmstadt-Center, the club changed its name in 1988 to CPA-Darmstadt-Center, (CPA standing for Christian Pathfinders of Adventist Youth). Club leader Toni Oblaski created the name. In 1992 all German clubs began to use the CPA form of the Pathfinder name.

Oblaski began the CPA-Darmstadt-Center club with only 12 Pathfinders and 30 leaders, the latter between the ages of 16 and 53. Eighty-five percent of the Pathfinders came from non-Adventist homes. "Our target is to give young people guidance for a life with Jesus Christ, making Him the center of their lives. Pathfindering gives us a chance to bring the gospel to young people whom we would not otherwise reach," Michael Franzke, a club leader, explained.

Since 1983 the club has participated in nearly every international camp hosted by the Euro-Africa Division. In 1987 the CPA at Darmstadt-Center and the CPA of Marienhöhe started an annual Pathfinder camp for the Central Rhenish Conference. Usually 80 participants attend, but in 1998 the number swelled to nearly 750.

Pathfinders in Germany are expertly trained in pioneer and survival skills. Each year clubs participate in winter camps and survival tours. They have even built towers and bridges. The highest tower built by the Darmstadt-Center club was 80 feet, with the highest platform 55 feet.

All of their activities, however, are not as physically rigorous. The club developed a musical team in 1993 under the leadership of Miriam Oblaski. Since 1994 the group has directed the music programs of conference CPA camps. A highlight for the team was their music arrangements for the children's Sabbath school programs at the General Conference Session in 1995 at Utrecht.

Service is an important part of all Pathfinder and youth ministries. Germany's Pathfinders have developed a system to support other groups in the area with their Pathfinder Day events, especially groups new to Pathfindering. The Darmstadt-Center musical team, for example, helps to arrange music for Pathfinder Days at area churches, and to conduct morning and afternoon activities such as slide shows.

The Panthers, CPA-Einöd/Saar, Germany

The Panthers of the Central Rhenish Conference in the South German Union Began in the 1970s when a former youth pastor gathered young people in the district to meet for Pathfinder lessons and religion classes in Neunkirchen-Saar. In 1986 a Pathfinder group formed in Einöd with 10 children. Sibylle Harth and Vincenzo Rizzo assumed leadership of the Einöd group in 1992. By then many of the Adventist members had either outgrown or showed no more interest in Pathfindering. The few remaining members began to invite their non-Adventist friends to the meetings. Today, the club, a mixture of Adventist and non-Adventist young people, has about

15 members.

In 1993 Sibylle left for Canada and the group reorganized as the Panthers. Although the group is smaller, the young people participate in many outreach programs. In 1995 the Panthers were the first overseas club to create a Web site with the help of Jeff Hamstra, a layperson in Texas. Through their Web site they share activities with local Scout clubs and witness to non-Adventist young people.

The Panthers also participate in the annual FronleichnamsLager-Corpus Christi Day Camp, formerly the PfingstLager Pentecostal Camp. It is the largest conference-wide camp-meeting in Germany, with more than 700 Pathfinders in attendance.

Himmelstuermer, Christlichen Pfadfinder der Advent-Jugend Kassel

A sculpture by artist Jonathan Borofsky, created as part of the Dokumenta IX in 1992, was the inspiration for the Kassel, Germany, Pathfinder club's chosen name, Himmelstuermer, meaning "man walking to the sky." (Dokumenta, one of the world's largest exhibits for modern art, takes place in Kassel every five years.) The city of Kassel is located almost in the middle of Germany with a population of around 200,000 and an Adventist congregation of 250 members.

The Kassel Pathfinder club began in 1970.

At that time the church called Pathfinders in Germany Jungfreunde (young friends), and the clubs operated on the principle of "learning by doing." The first club leader was Richard Grebe, fondly referred to as Uncle Richard, The next nearest club is Die Turmfalken (the kestrels [a type of falcon]), located southeast of Kassel in the city of Korbach.

The majority of the 28 Kassel Panthers Club members are Adventist, except 20 percent of the Junior Pathfinders. The club participated in the Euro-Africa Division international camporee in southern France in 1981 and 1986 and in the 1993 camporee for German-speaking countries—Switzerland, Austria, and Germany. For the past 10 years, the Panthers have participated in Germany's annual conference camporee, Frola. Held in the spring, 70 clubs from the German states of Hessen, Rheinland, Pfalz, and Saarland gather for the event. In autumn the Panthers conduct a weeklong hike through the mountains of central Germany. Their 1998 hike took them through Rennsteig in the German state of Thueringen. The 105-mile route followed a relatively high path between two rivers—the Werra and the Saale.

The Panthers, like many German clubs, do not perform some of the American Pathfinder rituals such as roll calls or singing the national anthem. But, as the Pathfinders throughout the world, their experiences and memories are filled with knot tying, compass reading, camping, music, discussion groups, crafts, Bible workshops, club outings, games, sports, hiking, orienteering, and national and international campouts.

Latvia is one of the newest countries to include Pathfindering in the church structure. In 1998 Mrs. Gune Rimane brought its first club with its fancy maroon and black uniforms to the Trans-European Division camporee in Norway. What they experienced so excited the Latvian youth that they began immediately to train staff and plan a national camporee with the help of Robert Holbrook. Clubs have sprung up over the country, and the idea has spread to the other two Baltic countries.

Euro-Asia

In 1991 a group of Pathfinders came from the United States to Lvov City in Ukraine. Youth ministry leaders from all of the conferences in the Ukrainian Union also gathered there to study and explore the development of the Pathfinder program in that area. The next year two teachers from Fridensau Seminary in Germany visited the Bukovinskaya Conference in Ukraine to conduct seminars for children and youth ministries. The seminars again introduced the Pathfinder program.

Then in 1994 the Ukrainian Union Conference (UUC) youth ministries director attended the Pathfinder camporee in the United States. This event further encouraged the development of the Pathfinder programs in the UUC, and as a result, clubs organized in the Eastern, Bukovinskaya, Western, Central, and Southern conferences.

By 1997 five more clubs had formed in the Podolskaya Conference. Presently the Euro-Asia Division (ESD) has 28 clubs with almost 350 members. ESD's goal has been to translate Pathfinder materials for their unions to further educate and encourage club development.

Africa

Africa may have more Pathfinders than any other continent, but the different ways of collecting statistics used in various areas make an exact count difficult to tally. Although we may not know exactly how many there are, we do know that they are active.

At least one church in Zambia has named a 17-year-old former Pathfinder as its first elder. Two small Pathfinders in Tanzania selected a tavern as a place to evangelize. They walked into the nearest tavern and spoke to a drunken woman. Soon they began Bible studies with her, and a few months later she was baptized. "No one had ever shown an interest in my well-being before!" the woman said afterward.

A 15-year-old girl in Malawi has memorized about 90 percent of the Bible. She can recite whole chapters and includes different voice inflections to indicate the various characters that may be speaking in it.

Civil warfare disrupted Pathfindering in Angola for several generations. Then in 1994 a young Brazilian couple working for ADRA—Paulo and Edra Lopez—organized a club in the capital of Luanda. The club immediately registered with UNHCR (United Nations High Commission for Relief) as a volunteer organization. UNHCR asked the club to participate in distributing the first food airlifted into the interior during a temporary lull in the fighting.

In 1996 the Lopezes transferred to ADRA Mozambique. There they also began organizing a Pathfinder Club in the capital of Maputo. Then they trained pastors from the interior to spread the concept. By 1999 they held a first national camporee with participants from all over the war-torn country.

Pathfinders in Africa love to march and rival the Brazilians for the most elaborate drill routines.

The Caribbean

Pathfinders in the Caribbean, especially the island of Barbados, have experienced rapid growth, averaging 5 percent each year. The Caribbean Pathfinders in Barbados boast 35 clubs and more than 700 Pathfinders. On December 13-15, 1996, they hosted a Pathfinder congress, and in 1997 held their first major island camporee at Bath, St. John, at-

Martha Yeseya from Malawi memorized 90 percent of the Bible.

tended by 9 clubs and 180 Pathfinders.

A division camporee held in Puerto Rico in 1998 reported 21,146 voice of junior youth campaigns and similar projects, resulting in baptisms for the year of 56,986. Twelve young boys and girls represented their fellow young preachers by speaking at the camporee.

The country of Antigua/Barbuda estimates that 10 percent of its population is Seventh-day Adventist. Pathfinders equal 10 percent of the total church membership, so 1 percent of the nation's population are Pathfinders. The deputy prime minister commented, "I wish all the country's youth could go through the Pathfinder program. It's the best plan I've seen for combating today's problems among children through a totally positive approach."

Southern Asia

Nature has displayed colorful backdrops for thousands of Pathfinder events through the decades and will for years to come. The April 18, 1993, all-island camporee sponsored by the Seventh-day Adventist Church in Sri Lanka at the Mirigama Boy Scout campsite was no different. Stately trees waved and bowed while flying squirrels glided from tree to tree, as if to welcome their 100 Pathfinder guests. Sri Lanka church president Peter Cooper commenced the camporee with a devotional presentation, and energetic, eager Pathfinders, wearing their uniforms with special camp scarves and badges, engaged in activities that brought them closer to their Master Counselor, Jesus Christ.

Have you ever heard of train evangelism? Pathfinders from Spicer Memorial College in Pune, India, boarded an express train on December 6, 1997. It was an exciting day for the Spicer group, the first time such a unique style of evangelism had been organized by the Pathfinders. The club sang gospel songs to the passengers; distributed 850 magazines, 10,000 tracts, and 500 stickers printed with the advent message; and enrolled 208 passengers in Voice of Prophecy and Health courses—all in an hour's time.

Where did they get such bold confidence? They practiced by conducting prayer meetings for Spicer College staff on campus and in faculty homes prior to their witnessing campaign. As a result, Spicer Pathfinders got to see—up close and personal—God's miraculous hand at work.

A young girl from another club in India attended a state-run school. When she refused to take her exams on Sabbath, her teachers asked that she present her reasons to the rest of the class. Her speech so impressed the teacher that

Pathfinders from Spicer Memorial College witnessed to passengers on Indian trains.

Train evangelism by the Patherfinders of Spicer Memorial College, Pune, India

hearts in worship and fellowship. Among them were J. J. Aitken, MV secretary of the Southern European Division; E. L. Minchin, MV secretary of the Northern European Division; and W. Raecker, MV secretary of the Central European Division. The event set a pattern for Pathfindering for the decades ahead.

More recently 1,500 Pathfinders from more than a dozen countries attended a camporee at Kopparbo, Sweden, with the theme "Christ Unites." The youth tried to outdo one another in fund-raising for a church building project in Albania. They raised more than $9,000.

she assigned the class a field trip to the Pathfinder girl's church the next Sabbath.

Hong Kong has had a small but enthusiastic program going for many years. One of their favorite pastimes is drilling and marching. It really paid off at the Oshkosh, Wisconsin, fiftieth anniversary camporee when they won first place in the drill meet. They received publicity in both the local Wisconsin papers and newspapers back in Hong Kong.

Europe

One of the most memorable events in the history of Pathfinders was the July, 1951, Paris Congress at Exposition Park, in Paris, France. Six thousand Adventist young people and their leaders came from 25 countries to unite their

World Club Feature:
Stoke Newington Pathfinder Club

The Stoke Newington Club, which began in the 1990s, began to lose its zeal. But with determination and a love for youth, club leader Roger Taffe brought the group to life again. "I observed that the children in our church were not being channeled and were basically thought to be unruly. I felt that a [Pathfinder] team, along with God's help, could make a difference," he explained.

Wearing the traditional Pathfinder khaki green, with yellow scarves, the club participated in the Trans-European Division's July, 1998, Camporee in Halsnes, Norway. Club members met people from all over the world and were able to observe many cultures. Their latest craze was aircraft modeling, and they hoped to develop this activity into a flying club in the near future.

Bermuda has nine churches, each with its own Pathfinder club. The Bermuda Conference, under the leadership of Pathfinder director Roy Butler, strongly supports them. When asked about the clubs' purpose and goals, Butler responded, "The Pathfinder club is a church-centered recreational and spiritual program that offers action, adventure, challenge, and group activities that produce team spirit and loyalty to our church. Our programs are attractive and active, which appeals to that restless age group. It provides a key step in the educational portion of their lives, taking them out of a classroom setting into outdoor adventure."

According to Butler, Bermuda's Pathfinder organizations seek to lead young people to understand that the church loves, cares for, and appreciates them: to show Pathfinders what God has planned for their lives; to develop their appreciation for nature and the environment; to teach them leadership skills and train them for missionary service; and to help them achieve a balanced physical, mental, social, and spiritual life.

"We have local camporees every year when the nine clubs get together for a fun, spirit-filled weekend on Darrell's Island," Butler says. The clubs have such colorful names as the Devonshire Bluebirds, the Somerset Cardinals, the Hamilton Pioneers, the Southampton Poincianas, the Midland Heights Trailblazers, the St. George's Cahows, the Pembroke Golden Leopards, the Warwick Longtails, and the St. David's Mariners.

Perhaps one of the most remote Pathfinder clubs is on St. Helena Island in the mid-Atlantic. Pitcairn Island in the remote South Pacific has had a club since 1964.

Approximately 1 million Pathfinders in 90 percent of the nations worldwide belong to thousands of clubs around the world.

CHAPTER SEVEN

KING JESUS THE SAVIOUR'S COMING BACK!

Discover the Power Camporee

Everyone loves celebrations, and Pathfinders are no exception. Pathfindering celebrated its fiftieth birthday in 1999 with the largest NAD-sponsored international camporee in the history of Pathfinders, held August 10-14. At Discover the Power camporee, more than 22,000 people from North America and more than 40 different countries, including 5,000 adult volunteer staff, and 17,000 Pathfinders, converged on Oshkosh, Wisconsin, to wish Pathfindering a happy golden anniversary. The event took place at the 275-acre campground of the Experimental Aircraft Association (EAA). The North American Division Pathfinder Ministries Department sponsored the camporee, and a board representing various segments of the NAD Pathfinder infrastructures, as well as conference, union, and NAD administrators, organized it.

Planning for Discover the Power International Camporee began in 1996. Countless numbers of dedicated Pathfinders, volunteers, employees, and corporate sponsors worked both before and during the event to make it happen. Eight hundred full-time volunteers served on the medical team, at the post office, and in food service, registration, lost and found, public relations, traffic control, security, and many other vital operations. Eighty people worked on the nightly programming, and it took a crew of 40 people two full days just to build the main stage.

With more than 70 activities and 65 educational honors classes daily to choose from, plus the exciting, spirit-filled evening programming that included music, drama, the testimonies of spiritual celebrities, and life-changing, Bible-based messages, the young people had never a dull moment at Discover the Power. The experience made a difference in the lives of not only those who attended, but on the Oshkosh community as well.

Ron Whitehead, executive director of Discover the Power, described the experience this way: "The DTP Camporee began as a dream to gather youth together at the largest five-day Seventh-day Adventist youth event in the world to:

1. **Praise and worship God**
2. **Teach outdoor skills**
3. **Blend different cultures and nations**
4. **Show off to the Oshkosh community that Seventh-day Adventist Pathfinders are a positive youth movement in their communities.**

"We prayed for a *safe* event. We prayed for a Spirit-filled event. We prayed that all the evening and daily programming would help Pathfinders of all ages to discover the power of Jesus Christ. What we are hearing from community leaders and from Pathfinder leaders is that the mission *was* accomplished. We all discovered the power of the True Master Guide, Jesus Christ."

And Pathfinders weren't the only ones who discovered God's power. Dorothy Opp, secretary of the Rocky Mountain Conference Youth Department, related the following story: "On the way home from the camporee a couple stopped to eat in a restaurant in Shawnee, Kansas. During the meal they became acquainted with a couple at a nearby table. In the course of the conversation the subject of God came up. The man at the other table said, 'I was an atheist until last Friday.' When he was asked what happened, here's what he said:

"'I live in Oshkosh, Wisconsin. Last week a group of about 20,000 kids camped at the EAA. These kids were all in tents! A huge storm was approaching. Some of the hail was baseball-sized. If it had hit them, they would have been killed! But just before the storm got there, it split and went right around them. It was a miracle! It had to be God protecting them. I can no longer believe that God does not exist. He showed me His power.'

"The man's wife then commented that the family had been praying for many years for his conversion."

The following story shared by Terry Dodge, director of DTP facility operations and director of volunteers, also testifies of God's love and power to care for His people:

"In 1994 at the Dare to Care Camporee it was important for the campers to drink lots of water because of the dry and hot climate in Denver, Colorado. I believe that on Sabbath it was 104 degrees. As a result, a large number of Pathfinders became sick because they did not drink enough water, creating a real problem to the medical team.

"As we laid plans for the Discover the Power Camporee, Ron Whitehead, Vern Byrd, and others began thinking about the problems of Sabbath drinking water. In March 1999 Vern became aware of a supply of bottled water. He found it was available for the cost of shipping and requested two semitrailers (50,000 bottles) of water. The miracle was that the water had been prepared for a company that decided not to take it and so the bottling company needed to find someone to take the water. The Lord provided that home at DTP Camporee.

"The water arrived in Oshkosh in July and went into storage. The camporee had it delivered to the camporee site on Friday afternoon and evening. Following the meeting on Friday the staff placed the water at various entrances to the assembly area to have it available for campers on Sabbath. They also took some to the first-aid station, so there would be a supply there for their needs.

"The Lord knew we needed the water long before the camporee and provided it to save many of the Pathfinders from getting sick. As He provided the water for the children of Israel in the wilderness, so He provided the water for His children [Pathfinders] today."

THE STORY IN PICTURES

Camporee Daily Activities/Highlights • Special Events
• Community Service • Evening Program Highlights

Photo courtesy of Georgia-Cumberland Conference (Dan Clifford, pilot; Jamie Arnall, photographer)

Camporee Daily Activities/Highlights

Pathfinders from Mexico relax after another fun-filled day at the Discover the Power Camporee. Photo by Felicia Ford.

Camporees make their own news—and newspapers!

The South Central Conference archway going up. Each conference at the camporee made an entrance to their own campsites.

Two Pathfinders enjoy a refreshing treat outside the information booth.

Chrissie Pangborn and Lacci Turk of the Redding Rangers smile for the camera.

Friends jostle for position at the communal water trough.

The tire portion of the obstacle course.

The camporee was a great place to make friends.

Sumo wrestlers throw their weight around outside one of the airplane hangars.

Dressed in uniform for another exciting day. Photo by Tompaul Wheeler.

The Ephesus Trail Blazers enjoy the camporee.

Up, up, and away! Lyssa Whatly makes climbing the rope ladder on the obstacle course look easy. Photo by Scott McPherson.

Pathfinders try the challenges of Sumo wrestling.

Members of the Northeastern Conference march to the beat of a different Drummer.

If you didn't have a golf cart, you had to cover the vast campground on foot.

Pathfinders in full regalia show off their skills in the precision drill competition.

Two gladiators, in lots of padding, battle it out in the ring.

Two friends race each other in the bungee run. This was one of the many fun activities available to Pathfinders during free time.

Three young Pathfinders show their enthusiasm for the camporee.

Justin Jagirdar smiles as he shows off his vest of pins.

Jenna Ramsay of the Nashua Nighthawks travels carefully across the rope bridge portion of the obstacle course. Photo by Scott McPherson.

Scott Houghton performs live in the Teen Barn. The barn also featured drama groups, games, and other activities sponsored by the YouthNet eXtreme Team.

Special Events

A radio-controlled plane prepares for takeoff. Photo by Scott McPherson.

A Pathfinder stands proudly with his model airplane. Photo by Scott McPherson.

Cessna 182 Commissioning Ceremony. On Sabbath afternoon, August 14, missionary pilot and nurse Marcio and Jane Costa, along with North American Division president, Alfred McClure, and thousands of spectators, participated in a dedication ceremony of the Cessna 182 aircraft that Pathfinders had helped to refurbish during the week. Following the ceremony, the Costas took off and headed for Guyana. The plane would transport medical supplies to remote areas of the country.

Tornado Evacuation. An unplanned (and scary) event on Thursday night demonstrated the awesome power of God's protection during the camporee. A tornado headed straight for the campground forced campers to take shelter in the airplane hangers. An EAA employee, who was amazed when the storm diverted and turned another direction, said to Pathfinder leader Merlin Cochran of Texas, "Your God must be an awesome God." Commenting on the occurrence, camp director Ron Whitehead said, "I believe that the storm obeyed the command of God to slide to the north and not hit us head-on."

The following day a group of Pathfinders from Denver, Colorado, were grocery shopping. When one of the group's leaders asked permission from the store manager to use a courtesy discount card for in-store specials, the manager responded, "The Lord parted the Red Sea for you guys last night. I guess I can let you use the courtesy card."

Community Service

During the Discover the Power camporee, Pathfinders could choose from 12 different community service projects to get involved with in and around the Oshkosh community. Sites and projects included the construction of the Little Oshkosh playground, clearing and remulching trails at the Evergreen Retirement Center, prairie restoration at Omre Prairie and Gromme, an ADRA clothing collection project, constructing walking trails at the Menesha Army Corps, cleanup and beautification at the Village of Winneconne, building

Danielle Johnson and Shaquinna Thomas of the Berea-Orion Pathfinders lend a hand at the Menesha Army Corps walking trail. Photo by Kelli Gauthier.

Dustin Ford, Carmen Bell, and Chris Armantrout of the Ridgetop, Tennessee, Ridgerunner Pathfinder Club help refinish the surface of the Little Oshkosh playground. Photo by Kelli Gauthier.

Members of the Berea-Orion Pathfinder Club of Boston, Massachusetts, pull together to help fix up the walking trails at the Army Corps. This was one of the community service projects that took place at the camporee. Photo by Kelli Gauthier.

brush piles and habitats for wildlife at Pheasants Forever, and working in the garden at the Paine Arts Center.

"You wouldn't believe the impact these community service projects have made," said Sam Bass of the Fox Valley SDA Church in Wisconsin. "People [from the community] are now contacting the church. What it's done for the church here has been fantastic." The bus drivers who transported the Pathfinders to and from their sites remarked at how well-behaved and polite the kids were.

Members of the Dunlap, Tennessee, Panthers deliver the first Bibles to Project Word. The club exceeded their goal of collecting 10 Bibles per person. Their 27 members collected 337 Bibles to send to countries overseas.

Evening Program Highlights

DTP Theme Song. Two Pathfinders, Valerie Jean Gonzales, and Kristen La Madrid, from the Glendale, California, Filipino Pathfinder Club, composed the camporee theme song, "Discover the Power of the Lord." The song, whose lyrics were based around the themes of the Discover the Power nightly programs, had been selected from among 16 entries in the song-writing contest. "The most powerful discover we can find is the power of the Lord and His love for us. So we decided to write our song about it," Valarie said. "We wanted the Pathfinders to be able to leave the camporee with a love for Him, something that would never die."

Kenny Rogers and The Neighborhood lead out in song service at one of the evening meetings.

Valerie Jean Gonzales, 15, and Kristen La Madrid, 14, had the opportunity to hear their own song sung by more than 17,000 Pathfinders. The girls were the winners of the Camporee theme song contest.

"Oshkosh is a very special place for me and my family. Even before I was born I attended my first EAA fly-in at Oshkosh. I have not missed a single one since. I was so excited when I heard that there would be a baptism on the EAA grounds at DTP. Just as EAA and Oshkosh have always been a part of my life, I wanted to have Jesus always be a part of my life. My baptism at DTP signified my connection with the Power Source. With Jesus as my pilot, I can safely fly to my home in heaven."—Julianna Weitzel.

"Jesus had been working in my heart a long time. He had been speaking to me through various individuals. Our former pastor, Elder White, had presented several mes-

World War II hero Desmond T. Doss attended the camporee. He received the Congressional Medal of Honor for saving the lives of many of his comrades while serving as a medic in the Army.

sages that touched me.

"During NET '98 Pastor Dwight Nelson asked for those who wanted to commit their lives to Jesus to come forward. Our family was watching the program at home. I just felt in my heart that this was the right thing to do. It's kind of like in the Bible where it says, 'This is the way walk ye in it.' Anyway, I asked my mom, 'How can I do this at home with a TV?'

She said God knew our hearts, and if we wanted to show our commitment to the rest of the family, we could stand up by the TV. Both of my siblings and I went forward. It was an easy step from there to Oshkosh. I, like my sister, have attended all the EAA fly-ins since before we were born. There are so many object lessons in flying that can teach us about our walk with Jesus. I thought it would be neat to have a place that already held such meaning for me take on an even greater significance. Besides, when my family and I visit each year, it will be an annual reminder of my commitment to Jesus."—Christina Weitzel

Being baptized at the DTP Camporee only seemed natural for Andrew Whitlow, age 10, of Syracuse, New York. Having been raised with Pathfindering parents, now in their thirty-sixth year of Pathfindering, Andrew was a mere 8 weeks old on his first Pathfinder backpack trip. When he was 8 months old he went to the Friendship Camporee and at age 5 he attended the Dare to Care Camporee in Colorado. He really looked forward to being a real Pathfinder at DTP in Oshkosh.

After having watches his dad (who is youth director of the New York Conference) baptize his best friend at a Southern Union Camporee, Andrew started thinking about his own baptism. He told his dad that he wanted to study carefully all of the lessons so that he could understand, before baptism, what a Seventh-day Adventist believes. So during the spring and summer of 1999 Andrew and his father studied together diligently, looking forward to the special camporee ahead. Family and friends gathered from several states for the special event. It was a great family reunion that they all enjoyed. But even more important, Andrew looks forward to the greatest reunion of all—heaven! (Story shared by Andrew's mother, Lisa Whitlow.)

On Sabbath afternoon, August 14, missionary pilot and nurse Marcio and Jane Costa, along with North American Division president, Alfred McClure, and thousands of spectators participated in a dedication ceremony of the Cessna 182 aircraft that Pathfinders helped to refurbish during the camporee. Following the ceremony, the Costas took off for the South American country of Guyana to provide a much-needed medical aircraft for reaching remote villages.

Willie Oliver, NAD Pathfinder Ministries director, sums up the Discover the Power experience: "Discover the Power Pathfinder Camporee was more than an event for Pathfinders in North America and around the world—it was an experience of a lifetime. It is the kind of unforgettable encounter in the lives of young people that makes a hefty deposit in the bank of relationships with Jesus and with the Seventh-day Adventist Church. For me it was the spot where Jessica and Julian, my two children, affirmed their faith in Jesus Christ through baptism. It was a witness to the Oshkosh community, and to a good bit of Wisconsin, about the ministry and mission of the Seventh-day Adventist Church."

Pathfinder clubs attending Discover the Power came from: Cameroon, Tanzania, Uganda, Zimbabwe, Zambia, Kenya, Czech Republic, Germany, Italy, Romania, Barbados, Cuba, Bahamas, Virgin Islands, Leimaco-N. Antilles, Cayman Islands, Columbia, Dominican Republic, Guyana, Jamaica, Mexico, Puerto Rico, Japan, Taiwan, South Africa, Argentina, Dominica, Peru, Venezuela, India, Bangladesh, Guam, Indonesia, Philippines, Singapore, Australia, England, Finland, Holland, Brazil, United States, Canada, St. Croix, Antigua, Nigeria (information provided by Center for Youth Evangelism).

SEVENTH-DAY ADVENTIST CHURCH

CHAPTER EIGHT

EPILOGUE

Where Do We Go From Here?

We stand at the threshold of a new era. Certainly as we look back on the past 50 years of Pathfindering, we have much to be thankful for. God has truly blessed Pathfinder ministries as it prepares young people, through wholesome activity, to share the gospel message and prepare others to meet Jesus when He returns. Owing to their enriching experience as Pathfinders, many Seventh-day Adventist young people have met Jesus and grown and matured in the faith, and as adults, have become outstanding church leaders. Overall, Pathfindering has served well the youth of our church. Yet in spite of all that we have to rejoice about, we cannot afford to become complacent with our past success.

As we look ahead to the twenty-first century, my dream for this ministry is that we will become more community based. Pathfinders isn't just for Seventh-day Adventist youth. If we are truly to fulfill the organization's purpose, we must widen our vision to include others in our communities. We are living in a time when divorce, single-parenthood, and dual careers undermine the family. Most young people in today's world don't have the blessings of growing up nurtured by loving, caring adults. Children and teens in todays' culture face serious challenges—and things aren't getting any better.

Walt Mueller, an expert on teen culture, did an informal survey asking teens to list, in order, the five greatest pressures they face. One teen put worry about looks at the top of the list. Next came getting good grades in order to get into college. Third, fourth, and fifth were drinking, sex, and popularity. The young person's responses were pretty typical. Add to those issues the realities of living in a home with no father (statistics say one third of the children in the United States fit this category) in a society where materialism, negative peer pressure, lack of moral values, family violence, and crime are standard fare. When you take a good look at today's world, it's a wonder that any child—Adventist or not—can survive unscathed. Yet as bleak as the picture may appear, there is a positive side. Here is a wonderful opportunity for Pathfinder ministries to fill a void in the dark and often frightening world of a child or teen who doesn't know Jesus and whose family life is shattered.

It is my sincere belief that this ministry will remain relevant for the twenty-first century only as we touch the lives of those around us, continually seeking new and innovative ways to meet their needs. Pathfinders will survive and thrive only as we remain relevant to the children and youth culture of our day—not by compromising spiritual principles, but by developing new modalities, "new wineskins" for the new vision. It is imperative that we do so in order to communicate the gospel in an effective manner.

Two thousand years ago Jesus gave us some directives. We know them well. He said, "Salt is good, but if it loses its saltiness, how can you make it salty again? Have salt in yourselves, and be at peace with each other." (Mark 9:50, NIV). Salt serves a multitude of purposes. It gives flavor to bland food and preserves, heals, and cleanses. When Jesus told us that we are to be salt, He meant that we are to season the world with His love and care for us. We are to heal brokenness and preserve against death and decay. And wherever there is sin we are to offer the cleansing that only Jesus can give.

I can't help thinking that as He uttered those words so long ago that Jesus was spanning the millenniums, looking tenderly at you and me in the here and now, and realizing that the world needs the benefits of salt more than ever. Then and now Jesus is saying to us, "Look around you. See the hurting people. They need Me. And I have commissioned you to tell them the good news that I love them. I'm coming soon for you and for them—much sooner than you think. Think about little Johnny down the street who has no dad. His mom works two jobs and can't afford to pay a baby-sitter. Johnny gets into mischief because he has no supervision. His friends have already introduced him to drugs. He's learned to steal money from his mother to support his habit. And unless someone intervenes it won't be long until he and his friends are experimenting with worse things. Where will it all end?

"But Johnny is my child," Jesus tells us. "He's gifted and talented. If only a loving, caring Pathfinder leader could guide and nurture those gifts. If only the Christian friends and positive role models that he finds through the local Pathfinder club could enrich his life. I can see Johnny now, marching in step with the drum corps. He looks good. I see him canoeing down the river, having a great time at the Pathfinder camporee. I see him working on his knot-tying honor at the weekly Pathfinder club meeting. And best of all, I see him one day coming down the aisle in church and giving his heart to Me. Can't you see it too?"

All around us we encounter sad stories of Johnny and others like him. How will they end? Will Johnny grow up to become a drug addict and repeat the cycles of broken family relationships? Or will someone extend a loving hand and invite him to something better? Will the Seventh-day Adventist children who live down the street from Johnny ask him to join them even when his behavior presents a challenge to their Christian experience? Will that leader who reaches out to Johnny with patience and understanding be you? I certainly hope so.

This is the model that we must follow. To do anything otherwise is to lose our savor, and as we all know, salt without savor is worthless. This is our challenge as we face the twenty-first century. We've come a long way and have only a little farther to go. Pathfinder ministries can be a blessing to the world, a vehicle for change, and a haven for youth desperately in need of guidance and stability in a world crumbling around them. My challenge to you today and for the future is to catch the vision—the same vision that inspired those who, with a pioneering spirit, forged the way for the development of Pathfinder ministries, but now modified and sharpened to meet the needs of the society we now live in. As we look back on the past with joy and satisfaction, let's keep focused on the thought that

the best and most fruitful days of Pathfindering
are still to come!

—*Willie Oliver*
   Director of Pathfinder Ministries
   North American Division of the Seventh-day
   Adventist Church